Accelerated Learning

Photographic Memory: Simple, Proven Methods to Remembering Anything, Speed Reading: How to Read a Book a Day, Mindfulness: 7 Secrets to Stop Worrying

By

Ryan James

© **Copyright 2018 by Ryan James**

All rights reserved.

The following book is reproduced below with the goal of providing information that is as accurate and as reliable as possible. Regardless, purchasing this book can be seen as consent to the fact that both the publisher and the author of this book are in no way experts on the topics discussed within, and that any recommendations or suggestions made herein are for entertainment purposes only. Professionals should be consulted as needed before undertaking any of the action endorsed herein.

This declaration is deemed fair and valid by both the American Bar Association and the Committee of Publishers Association and is legally binding throughout the United States.

Furthermore, the transmission, duplication or reproduction of any of the following work, including precise information, will be considered an illegal act, irrespective whether it is done electronically or in print. The legality extends to creating a secondary or tertiary copy of the work or a recorded copy and is only allowed with express written consent of the Publisher. All additional rights are reserved.

The information in the following pages is broadly considered to be a truthful and accurate account of facts, and as such any inattention, use or misuse of the information in question by the reader will render any resulting actions solely under their purview. There are no scenarios in which the publisher or the original author of this work can be in any fashion deemed liable for any hardship or damages that may befall them after undertaking information described herein.

Additionally, the information found on the following pages is intended for informational purposes only and should thus be considered, universal. As befitting its nature, the information presented is without assurance regarding its continued validity or interim quality. Trademarks that mentioned are done without written consent and can in no way be considered an endorsement from the trademark holder.

All additional rights reserved.

Table of Contents

Book - I: Speed Reading: How to Read a Book a Day - Simple Tricks to Explode Your Reading Speed and Comprehension

Speed Reading.. 5

Introduction 6

Chapter 1: Understanding Speed Reading. 7

Chapter 2: History of Speed Reading 10

Chapter 3: Reading vs Speed Reading 11

Chapter 4: What's Your Speed-Reading Level?   13

Chapter 5: Debunking Myths about Speed Reading 15

Chapter 7: Breaking Poor Reading Habits 22

Chapter 8: Speed Technique: Make Your Eye Move Faster   27

Chapter 9: Comprehension Technique: Skimming+30

Chapter 10: Retention Technique: Maintain Focus 32

Chapter 11: Keys to Speed Reading Success 35

Chapter 12: Read a Book a Day - Speed Reading Exercises You Can Start and Make Into a Habit................37

Chapter 13: Speed Reading Tips that Enhance Your Habits   40

Chapter 14: Eye Exercises for Speed Reading 45

Conclusion 47

Book - II: Photographic Memory: Simple, Proven Methods to Remembering Anything Faster, Longer, Better

Photographic Memory 48

Introduction 49

Chapter 1: Understanding the Memory... 50

Chapter 2: Photographic Memory 52

Chapter 3: Creative Thinking 54

Chapter 4: Visualization......................57

Chapter 5: Introduction to Memorization Techniques   60

Chapter 6: Peg Systems 64

Chapter 7: Emotion-based Memorization 71

Chapter 8: Mind Mapping 77

Chapter 9: Visualizing Names 82

Chapter 10: Visualizing Numbers (Major System) 87

Chapter 11: Visualizing Numbers (Other Systems) 94

Chapter 12: Memory Palace 100

Conclusion 105

Mindfulness 106

Book - III: Mindfulness: 7 Secrets to Stop Worrying, Eliminate Stress and Finding Peace with Mindfulness and Meditation

Introduction 107

Chapter 1: The 'Here' And 'Now' 108

Chapter 2: Reap the Benefits 111

Chapter 3: From Auto to Manual 115

Chapter 4: Cross Your Legs 117

Chapter 5: Squeezing Mindfulness In ... 124

Chapter 6: Overcoming the Obstacles ... 127

Chapter 7: Staying Behind the Wheel 129

Conclusion 131

Book - I

Speed Reading

- How to Read a Book a Day –

Simple Tricks to Explode Your Reading Speed and Comprehension

Introduction

Congratulations on purchasing the book, *"Speed Reading: How to Read a Book a Day - Simple Tricks to Explode Your Reading Speed and Comprehension"*.

Speed reading is the more efficient way to read and can bring you more benefits in life that you can ever imagine. You can go from good to great!

There are many misconceptions about speed reading that makes people apprehensive about learning this skill. But when you understand the benefits it can bring to your life, you will be more eager to learn how to do it. Speed reading will empower you, help maintain your focus, and increase your levels of comprehension.

You will be a more productive individual and still have time to enjoy other important things in life. Reading efficiently will allow you to acquire more knowledge which, in turn, makes you more creative, more innovative, and more successful.

Speed reading will give you the ability to read at least one book a day. Imagine how much information you can attain and retain! You can join the ranks of very successful people around the world who consider reading as an important tool to thrive in almost every area of life.

If you are already a reader, you will be surprised to know that speed reading will make that hobby a more enjoyable experience. It all starts with accepting that you may have poor reading habits that you need to get rid. This is so you can gain an understanding of speed reading techniques and how to apply them. In the following chapters, you learn more about how speed reading can work wonders for you.

It's never too late to learn a new skill. Start speed reading today!

Chapter 1: Understanding Speed Reading

A lot of people don't realize that reading is a skill that they often use. You read the news on paper or on the internet to see what's happening around you. You read books, letters, social media posts, recipes, and all kinds of notes during an average day. You read financial reports and business correspondence. You browse numerous emails from friends or colleagues at work. Do you realize how much reading you actually get done in one day?

You may think that it is enough knowing how to read and comprehend. But even if you are able to do the basics well, you can still improve your reading skill – and you should, since reading takes up a lot of time in your everyday life. Poor reading habits can be changed and unlearned to make you more efficient and more productive. This is where *speed reading* comes in.

Did you know that the average person can read approximately 200 to 250 words in a minute, or take about 2 minutes to read a page of a document? With speed reading, you can actually double your reading rate of words/minute. You can breeze through, and comprehend, any content in half the time! Imagine what you can do with the time you save! You can use it to complete other tasks, or just rest and relax.

The art of speed reading improves your comprehension skill by allowing you to have a "bigger picture" grasp of what you are reading. As a skill, this can be advantageous to your work or profession.

The Science of Reading

Before you proceed to mastering speed reading, you must first understand the way you read. Reading is a complex skill. Different people have different ways on how they make sense of letters and how they are put together. It is not true that you need both of your eyes to be focused on a specific letter within a word. Each eye can actually focus on different letters simultaneously, normally two characters away from each other. Your brain puts these images together and constructs the word. This process happens in an instant, so a reader can actually zip through many different texts at a given time.

There are many different categories of reading and these affect how fast a person reads. Before you get to speed reading, you have to understand that every person is wired differently based on how they were taught as well as other influences surrounding them. Typically, people learn to read when they begin school and they are commonly taught to do so word by word. Word by word reading causes the eyes to be fixated on only one word, sometimes the previous one, taking the reader back a step in reading and comprehension. This mechanical form of reading is rather slow, but this is the most common way through which people read and comprehend. Not everyone is informed that there is a more efficient way.

When you think about how much time is spent just looking at several words and concepts, reading may seem like a tedious and very mechanical process. There is *fixation* – basically staring at a word or a couple of words which usually takes a quarter of a second. Then one's eye will move to another word or set of words, the process is called *saccade*, and it takes a tenth of a second. Then the reader repeats the cycle and pauses about half a second to comprehend what he or she just read. These mechanical processes put together become the reason why an average person can read about only 200 to 250 words a minute.

The different types of reading are:

- *Mental reading*
- *Auditory reading*
- *Visual reading.*

Mental reading is also known as sub-vocalization. It is a way of reading wherein one sounds out every word internally, much similar to saying something to yourself. Mental reading is the slowest type of reading. Readers who practice mental reading can read to about 250 words a minute.

Auditory reading is a bit faster, as it requires the person to listen to every word that is read and not sound them out. Those who practice this usually read 450 words a minute.

The fastest type is visual reading. Instead of sounding out the words or hearing them, the reader comprehends what the word means by sight, making them read an average of 700 words a minute. Speed reading via visual reading is a skill you can master as you continually practice and train.

Now, speed reading can be very handy and valuable. However, it is safe to say that there are instances when using speed reading is not a good idea. There are reading materials that you should never speed read. You must know when and how to adapt a reading technique according to the material on hand.

In the following chapters you will discover the benefits of speed reading, its history and comparison to average reading as well as on how to develop and master speed reading so you can use it to your advantage.

Chapter 2: History of Speed Reading

It is good to understand how the concept of speed reading came about. The beginnings of speed reading was created through the use of the *tachistoscope*, a device used by the US Air Force to train their pilots' focus and memory. The gadget will show the pilot an image for a short period of time then remove it from view. The pilot would have to identify which are enemy planes while they simulate battles in the cockpit.

This *tachistoscope* methodology was later applied to reading: it flashed a group of words on a screen for .002 seconds and readers were tested if they remembered and understood the phrase completely.

In the beginning, it was believed that people read by looking at all the letters in a word then associating them with meaning. The concept of "reading by letters" was changed when it was proved, through studies and experiments, that people have the ability to read not just one word, but a group of three, five, or even more words at a given time. Thus, speed reading was popularized.

Evelyn Wood was the one who coined the phrase. She studied the habits exhibited by fast readers and developed techniques on how to enhance one's reading speed. She taught in schools and seminars. President John F. Kennedy, along with his brother Bobby, was schooled in her methods and became a strong advocate for speed reading during his term. President Jimmy Carter, his wife, and several White House staff similarly took speed reading courses.

Through the years, speed reading methodologies have been upgraded. However, the basic foundation – reading multiple words faster and with full comprehension – has not changed. You can apply latest developments in speed reading to go from being a good reader to becoming a great one.

Chapter 3: Reading vs Speed Reading

The skill of speed reading is not very different from average reading – the only thing is that it is a lot more focused. Average reading requires you to engage your senses (sight, hearing, speaking) and your brain. With speed reading, you need to utilize your brain power and these senses in even greater fashion so that you will be more focused and more efficient.

Here's how speed reading expands the natural way of reading:

1. **You *see* the words.**

    Initially you read a group of words (usually 3 to 5) at a glance. If they are words that you are familiar with, you don't have to read them one by one. Next, you magnify your vision and try to read and comprehend more words at a glance. Many well-practiced speed readers can easily see and process about 10 to 16 words. Then you magnify your vision to read line by line, horizontally and vertically, per page. Most good speed readers can easily see and process about 2 to 3 lines at once.

2. **You do *silent reading*.**

    Average readers sound out words as they read. This is okay for beginners but if you want to speed up, you will have to do away with it. Speed readers can read without the voice (not even a whisper in their mind) and just use their eyes and brain.

3. **You *decode* the words.**

    The mind decodes words that you fail to recognize. It breaks the words into syllables and tries to get the meaning then pronounce it. When you don't know what it means, you check the dictionary. An average reader will take a much longer time to read when they encounter unfamiliar words. As you read more material, you are introduced to more new words. You will eventually increase your speed reading rate whilst you also continue to expand your vocabulary. You will find it easier to decode words after that.

4. You *comprehend* the material.

Learning something and understanding it is the purpose of reading. It is not just seeing letters, words, phrases or sentences put together – it's about getting the whole thought, obtaining information and probably gaining new perspective. When it comes to speed reading, the level of your comprehension can be determined by the following concentration, extensiveness of your vocabulary, background of the subject matter, and reading speed.

Concentration: Whenever you read, you need to have concentration. Speed reading would require double the average amount of concentration you put into reading text. Your focus needs to be sustained because you see, decode and comprehend all at the same time and do so within a small amount of time. You need to be attentive to the main ideas so you can get a good grasp of your material.

Extensiveness of vocabulary: When you have a wide vocabulary, you will find it easier to understand the material you are reading. You will not have to stop and try to properly understand the meaning of a word or words from other sources. You can use your time to finish reading more material.

Background of subject matter: When you are already familiar with the material you are reading, you will have a head start with comprehending it fully – you understand key points, you get the jargon and style, and you know the main points to look for.

Reading speed: It is not just about reading fast – it is about reading wisely. It's all about perspective: a speed reader knows when they need to speed up and when they need to slow down and take his time. They would also know when to skim and when to focus more on weighty concepts. It depends on the type of reading and the material that they are reading. Not reading at the right speed will weaken your comprehension.

Chapter 4: What's Your Speed-Reading Level?

Before you begin to apply speed reading techniques, you need to know where you are right now as a speed reader. As with learning or trying out anything new, you need to make an honest evaluation of yourself so that you know where you must start and which areas you have to work on.

Readers fall into different categories based on how fast they read counted in *words per minute* (wpm). Find out what level speed reader you are:

IF YOU READ 1 to 200 WORDS PER MINUTE,

You are very likely a TALKER (translated: SLOW READER). This means that you read words at the same speed as you speak. Talkers usually practice sub-vocalization – you may even find yourself moving your lips as you read. Talking back or sounding out holds you back because you are hearing your voice in your head and you can't go any faster than the way you talk.

IF YOU READ 200 to 300 WORDS PER MINUTE,

You are considered an AVERAGE READER. You only probably read when you have to, and you won't take up reading as a hobby. While you are faster than a talker, since you can read a group of words at once, you may also be practicing vocalization. A lot of people are at this level.

IF YOU READ 300 to 700 WORDS PER MINUTE,

Consider yourself an ABOVE AVERAGE READER. You are someone who rarely vocalizes and you can read chunks of words at a glance while completely understanding the material. It is highly likely that your vocabulary is wide and you enjoy doing a lot of reading.

IF YOU READ MORE THAN 700 WORDS PER MINUTE,

You are a SPEED READER! You find yourself reading more than 10 words at a glance. You can read both vertically and horizontally without much problem. You have great comprehension. You not only enjoy reading, but you are very confident about your skill.

If you can read up to 16 words in one look and fully comprehend it, then you are a speed reader who doesn't need lessons at all. If you are a struggling reader, and you want to get better then read on. You will get practical tips on how to increase your level of speed and comprehension. If you are either average or above average, this book will help you enhance your skills further so that you can easily become a speed reader!

Chapter 5: Debunking Myths about Speed Reading

There are many misconceptions about speed reading and when you don't set things straight, you will have a harder time working on your level and improving your speed rate. After all, one reason for learning speed reading should be to bring enhancement to your reading ability as well as making reading a pleasurable and profitable experience for yourself.

You may think you have an idea of speed reading – and these ideas may not be right at all! It's perfectly normal. A lot of people have erroneous concepts of how to read fast and most of them are untrue.

Read on and find out the wrong ideas people have about speed reading. You don't have to be stuck with these myths. All you have to understand is that you only need to make slight adjustments to your established routines and habits, and you will be well on your way to becoming a speed reader.

- <u>Myth 1</u>

When you speed read, you don't enjoy reading.

This is false because speed reading actually allows you to read more efficiently. And when you read more efficiently – you not only save time, you also understand more! This means you get to enjoy reading more books, magazines, articles, blogs and other reading materials, print or online. A lot of people also pick up a love for reading once they learn how to speed read.

- <u>Myth 2</u>

When you speed read, you don't have to understand as well and as much as average reading.

This is untrue since speed reading requires a higher level of focus. When you concentrate well, you will also comprehend things better. With speed reading, you are able to read in context and understand better in the least amount of time.

- <u>Myth 3</u>

When you speed read, you skip words.

You don't skip anything when you speed read, the difference is that you no longer read the text word by word. Speed reading makes you read words in chunks or by line so you don't fixate your eyes on just one. You will understand faster when you read more words by line. But you don't miss out on any word.

- <u>Myth 4</u>

When you speed read, you need to move your finger across the text.

A guide or a pacer is a helpful tool when you begin to learn speed reading. You use it to mark where you are on the page to prevent regression and help you keep focus. You will learn more about meta guiding or using pacers in the succeeding chapters.

However, keep in mind that not all speed readers keep their fingers or a pencil as they go through pages quickly. Once you get the hang of it, you will be able to drop the pacer and speed read with ease.

Chapter 6: Benefits of Speed Reading

Speed reading offers plenty of benefits for everyone, this is especially so for business people, students, and for anyone who does a lot of reading.

You may be wondering why it is beneficial to spend time learning speed reading techniques despite your day being already full. Here's one reason: With the vast amount of information coming at you every day, investing a little time in learning strategies for faster reading makes sense.

Imagine zipping through your email inbox in half the time, efficiently going through the social media updates of your friends and responding quickly.

Speed reading is a technique that will allow you to comprehend more and increase the rate of your reading to double or even triple that of your current level. Once you acquire the ability, you will have the skill for life and enjoy its long-term benefits! Isn't that a sweet deal?

Here are some more reasons that will help you decide to start learning and improving on your speed reading skills:

1. **You will have develop better time management.**

   The old adage *time is* gold is so true. Everyone should use their time wisely because it is the most precious commodity you will ever have. Success largely depends on how you manage your time. With speed reading, you can save up time going through different materials to gain useful information and use that time to apply that knowledge you gained.

2. **You will be empowered.**

   First impressions and judgments are usually based on the words that leave a person's mouth. For example, being able to share your point of view or understanding of important facts in a business meeting will not only give you a boost of confidence but also a chance to impress other people with your knowledge. Having been able to speed read through pertinent documents (reading AND fully comprehending the contents) will give you knowledge power.

Another instance would be social situations. Having sped read news – whether it's about world events, social media, industry, entertainment, or even gossip – you will be able to hold conversations better with others and be comfortable with what you know.

3. You will be exposed to more opportunities.

Exponential growth comes as you read more and expand your knowledge. And as your speed reading improves, you will gain even more wisdom that will help you grow professionally and personally. This will open the door for many opportunities that you can take hold of.

Did you know that speed reading can help you get promoted or get you that high-paying job you have been eyeing? In today's competitive corporate world, you can stand out by getting advanced degrees, formal trainings or certifications. You can do these things online and speed reading can help you improve your educational background by managing these courses and accomplishing them in a shorter amount of time with great results.

Remember, when you increase your professional value, it translates to better opportunities for employment and income. This equates to more security and financial freedom.

4. You become more confident.

Speed reading can improve or strengthen your personality. If you are a person who is not comfortable speaking to colleagues or your boss, you will stay in the sidelines and have no confidence to really participate. However, if you keep abreast of what is happening within and around your company and industry, you will be able to make confident suggestions and proposals.

You can speed read through financial news, industry updates, and reports on what is going around the competition in the marketplace. You will also be able to answer questions confidently. Even when people disagree with your opinion, you will be comfortable and confident knowing that you have full comprehension of the topics you are discussing because you have read them well– through speed reading.

With improved self-confidence, you're also better at exercising self-control and make wiser decisions in the workplace.

5.   You will have better memory.

A lot of people can read through something and forget what they have read after a while. Speed reading techniques can increase your understanding of a topic or fact that you have come across. Your brain is wired to recall, with precision, concepts that you have good comprehension of. You can make your brain stronger and more efficient by training it through speed reading. When you improve your memory, you will also improve on your creativity.

6.   You will feel more relaxed.

People who read will tell you that it can be a very relaxing, stress-busting pastime. Whether you read slow or read fast, reading can relax your nerves and ease the worries out of your thoughts. Picking up and going through the right book at the right time can instantly change your mood or your whole perspective about a subject.

As you speed read, you will be able to go cover more material, absorb more information and generally feel more relaxed. In doing so, you will also be able to quiet the voices, noise and tension around you. This peaceful state can enhance your emotional and spiritual being, which brings positive results to your physical body.

Try speed reading for a month and you will begin to see a marked difference in your behavior and emotions.

7.   You will enhance your learning capabilities.

Speed reading is a way to enhance your focus. When you know how to give your full concentration on whatever task you are doing, you will get better at it – this applies not just to reading. You will have more interest on what you are doing and you can process information better and at a much faster rate. You will also be eager to grab at any chance to enhance your learning and creativity. Again, this paves the way to more opportunities.

8.   You will be more sophisticated with your thinking.

Science says that speed reading can positively affect the brain's neuroplasticity. The brain will be trained to chart new connections and allow you to think in a more complex and advanced manner.

9. You will have less stress.

Since speed reading trains you to focus, through it you would be able to increase your meditation skills. In today's world of information overload, people tend to multi-task and lose focus. Fragmented attention will make you inefficient and unproductive. Not getting tasks done, or attending to too many tasks at once, will bring you stress.

When you learn to focus, a skill acquired through speed reading, you will be able to complete tasks more efficiently and have much less stress because you know you're performing at your best.

10. You will be inspired to achieve or dream more.

With enhanced memory, focus, thinking, and creativity, you will find yourself aspiring for more. As the world around you becomes bigger, you will dare to dream bigger and go further. The benefits of speed reading skills are not limited to just reading and comprehension. It can affect your whole outlook in life.

11. You will be more innovative as a leader.

Speed reading can enhance your thought processes and make you a better leader. As a leader, you would be able to lead changes, expansion, and innovation confidently knowing that you have the right information and the skills to meet the goals you set.

You also become more creative at problem-solving as you engage your imagination. You can cross-pollinate concepts and make them more useful. You have the skill to implement the initiative as well. Who knows, the next billion-dollar idea may just come from you.

12. You become good at problem-solving.

Speed reading allows you to reframe problems by understanding key ideas and unlocking your imagination. Did you know that your subconscious is powerful? Studies indicate that the subconscious mind solves problems at 100,000 mph while the conscious mind can only go at a maximum of 150 mph.

How does speed reading help you solve problems faster? Speed reading gives you the skill to course more facts and figures to your subconscious. When the subconscious has more information, it can solve problems better. This is called logic training. When you speed read, you train your brain to be more efficient at receiving and understanding new information then connecting it to what is previously stored.

You will have enhanced logical thinking processes as you continue to enhance your speed reading since the connections that are needed for it gets activated. You will see the benefits of these enhancements to your thinking process in your everyday decision-making.

Chapter 7: Breaking Poor Reading Habits

As with developing other new skills, learning speed reading will require you to unlearn and break old reading habits that you have acquired over the years. You cannot become a speed reader when you still practice poor reading habits.

It is common for people to have one or two, or even more, poor or slow reading habits. When these habits are done away with, a person can make room for new and efficient habits in their life. First, you will need to understand the most common poor reading habits, see if you are practicing them, and learn what you can do to overcome them.

Remember, the goal of learning to read fast is more than just speed – it is to become more efficient at reading and comprehension.

1. Sub-Vocalization

As you learned in the early chapters, young readers were trained to pronounce every word in their heads or mutter under their breaths while they read. As they grew older, they began to develop an "inner monologue" going on in their minds whenever they read—this happens as a force of habit. Their reading speed is similar to how fast they talk. While it is conventional, sub-vocalization prevents a person from improving his reading speed.

Here is how sub-vocalizing can slow you down: the average talking rate of a person is 200 to 250 words per minute. When you sub-vocalize, you read at the same speed. While you have been previously trained to do so, you don't have to say or hear every word in your head in order to understand what you are reading.

When you train yourself to speed read, your mind can automatically process what you see so you don't have to stop and sound it out. You can improve your reading speed from the normal 200 to 250 words a minute to just about any level you decide.

In order to overcome this poor reading habit, *honesty is key*: you need to acknowledge that you actually have a voice in your head and that you should turn it off when reading.

The next step is to practice not speaking. Here are some tips on how to stop "saying or hearing words as you read" and kick that bad habit out of your life:

- *Don't read for sound.* This means that you read for meaning. It is a lot like listening. You hear words – but the voice is not yours – and your brain makes the connection of what the speaker (in this case, the author) is trying to send across. Listening while reading means you are reading for meaning. You are not looking for the sound so the words that you see are read as units of meaning.

- *Stop those lips from moving.* Chew gum so that your mouth has something to do other than sound out the words as you see them. By disengaging your vocal system, you will be able to "listen" and get the message without vocalizing what you see.

- *Quiet the inner reading voice.* This may take a bit of work but when you train yourself to do so, you will soon find yourself speed reading with ease. Perceive words instead of seeing them. Think of words as symbols instead of sound.

- *Take in more words.* When you widen what you see, you are making yourself read more words and your brain stops vocalizing. Speed reading is all about focus. Concentrate hard and find thought units and not words in sentences.

2. Word-by-Word Reading

This is about focusing on reading separate words instead of ideas. You can get the gist of a phrase or sentence in groups of words instead of taking it one by one. This makes comprehension difficult and people read even more slowly. The best way to break this habit is to learn how to properly chunk words together and get what they mean as a block. Look at this simple sentence: *Time is gold.* Did you read it word for word or as an idea? You can increase your vision span to absorb in more words and still understand the concept.

Creating blocks of words, also called "word-chunking", is a way to eliminate sub-vocalization. Chunking means you train your eyes to read a set of words at once. This way, you read faster. Try reading the following: *The quick brown fox jumps over the lazy dog.*

You can read it in blocks or phrases at a glance as: *the quick brown fox | jumps over | the lazy dog* by focusing on the words fox, jumps and dog. Overall, you understood what the sentence meant. When you read in chunks, you will cover more text, thus read faster.

You can take chunking up a notch by separating sentences or paragraphs and reading them by sections. Read one block as one concept, and do this for the rest of the page. After you're done you'll realize that you have read through the whole page faster. This exercise will take practice so challenge yourself to do it often until you feel comfortable and confident with it.

3.   Ineffective Eye Motion

As with reading word by word, when you don't use your peripheral vision to work your way across the text, you will be a slow reader. When your eyes are not trained to take in a lot of words or a whole line of text, you will read ineffectively.

Normally, your eye can see about an inch-and-a-half at a time – this means that it is possible to view up to five words at a glance. To overcome ineffective eye motion, you need to relax and expand your gaze. By doing so, you will not see a single word specifically, but blocks of words that hold meaning. Using your peripheral vision is the level that comes after chunking – reading a whole line instead of a small group of words.

To do this, you need to focus on the middle first then scan the rest of the line using your peripheral vision. Don't worry too much that you will skip a word – you won't. As you go through your material using this method, you will realize that you will cover more text and still understand everything you just read.

Remember that like other speed reading techniques, this will take practice, but you will be happy with the results. Learn more about improved eye fixations and how you can exercise your eye muscles in chapter 9 of this book.

4.   Regression

Skipping back to the words you have already read is called regression. This is a common practice of slow readers. When you worry about forgetting or misunderstanding a text then go back to read it again, you will most likely lose your focus and your reading flow.

When you regress, there is the danger of losing your comprehension of the whole subject. Re-reading can be counter-productive. Instead of flitting back and forth, train yourself to read in one smooth flow. You must be aware of this: only re-read the text when you absolutely need to. Otherwise, just proceed.

You can also be subconsciously regressing and wasting time. To avoid re-reading or reduce the amount of time you regress you can use a guide or pointer. As you move the pointer across the page, your eyes will naturally follow along. You will train your eyes to dodge skipping back and just follow the pointer. You can use your finger as a pointer.

Practice doing this so you can force yourself to not stop or go back. When you reach the end of your page, think about what you read. When you recall what you have just finished reading, without going back, it's a good start. Continue to practice reading this way until you get to the point that you don't have to use a pointer.

5. Poor Concentration

Here's a fact: poor concentration does not produce good results. When you try to read while watching television, you will find it hard to focus on reading. Even if you learn to turn off sub-vocalization and read by chunks, you will not have full comprehension with poor focus. Without concentration, the words will blur into each other.

If you want to be able to read fast and comprehend well, take away as much distraction as you can. Set up a conducive reading environment. Try to avoid multitasking as you read.

Distractions are not just external – there are also internal distractions such as going over events of the day in your mind or thinking about what to do next. Allowing your thoughts to wander will restrain your ability to comprehend. Go to *chapters 11 and 12* for tips on how to create the right reading environment that is essential to building your speed reading skills.

6. Practicing linear reading

The traditional linear reading is what most readers are trained to do: to read from left to right, across to down, from beginning to end. Non-linear reading is a reading technique that allows you to jump from one section to another, oftentimes not actually finishing a sequence.

While linear reading is acceptable, it could also mean that you are wasting time by paying attention to supplemental information. You can overcome this poor reading habit by doing things non-linearly.

The first thing you should do is search for the following: headlines, bullet points, headings, items in boldface/highlight and transitions. You can scan the contents quickly and identify what is important and what is supplemental. Don't waste time on fluff, but find key information.

Look for interesting and engaging points that authors usually put in – this will help you understand the point that the writer is trying to get across, so you don't have to go through the anecdotes, stories or accompanying examples that expand their concept.

You can choose to re-read or skip parts that you like. You can learn how to skim more effectively in chapter 10.

7. Not knowing how to skim

Skimming can be handy when it is crunch-time. When the teacher suddenly calls for a recitation or a pop quiz but you forgot to read through your lesson yesterday, or when your boss calls for a meeting and you only have 10 minutes to read through the reports, you need your speed reading skills.

You waste precious time and you don't get the necessary information when you don't know how to skim. Calm down, take a breath, open that book or report and read through it the right way. The key is to find the main points or headlines. You can go through the headings or the table of contents, then subtitles or captions. This will give you an overall feel of what the whole document or chapter is about.

After you go through the headings, read through the first paragraph, the last one and the middle part. Piece together what you got and when you have an idea, you can start reading the rest, if you still have time. This process will allow you to keep information better. There is a chapter in this book dedicated to skimming.

Chapter 8: Speed Technique: Make Your Eye Move Faster

A speed reader has greater comprehension when they read in chunks or phrases since there is stronger meaning conveyed. The eyes need to be still and focus in order to see something. When the eyes are moving around, the vision will be blurry. Speed reading is not just about moving your eyes quickly across the page, it is about having good focus while maintaining a wide span of vision.

It is also about improving fixation: how the eyes move and become still as you read, how it focuses on a group of words then proceed to the next after understanding the first one. The fewer fixations, the faster reading.

To understand how eyes fixate itself on words, try to read this:

A thing of beauty is a joy forever.

If you are a slow reader, you will read this sentence in 5 to 8 eye fixations – as your eyes go word by word. When you are a fast reader, you will have greater span of vision and be able to read this in two or four eye fixations only.

A *thing* | of *beauty* | is a *joy* | *forever.*

A thing of *beauty* | is a *joy* forever.

If you want to see how eye fixation works in action, you can ask a friend to observe you while you are reading or you can observe him. You will notice that the reader's eye will move from left to right in a fraction of a second then move again to the right. Once the reader gets to the end of the line, his eyes will go back to the left and start fixations all over again. Eye fixations vary depending on the length of the line he is reading, his familiarity with the subject and the breadth of his vocabulary.

Eye Fixations and Familiarity

Your background, education, and interest all factor into your rate of speed reading. Your knowledge of a topic will influence how fast you read per eye fixation. Reading about something that is in your field of expertise will allow you to read not just quickly but confidently. You are aware of jargon and the topic of interest. Compared to a grade-schooler, a finance consultant will read a business report or an investment proposal much faster and understand it better.

As you read and read, you will expand your knowledge. As you become familiar with more and more topics, you will read even faster. It works and benefits you both ways.

Eye Fixations and Vocabulary

The wider your vocabulary, the greater your word recognition will be as you read. This means you can take in more words in groups. Here is a good example of having limited vocabulary. Read the following and try to comprehend what the author is saying: *Sownynge in moral vertu was his speche, and gladly wolde he lerne, and gladly teche.*

This text is from The Canterbury Tales. When you are not familiar with these words, you will notice that it took you a longer amount of time to read it (you tried to read and understand it word by word) compared to reading this:

Filled with moral virtue was his speech, and gladly would he learn, and gladly teach.

When you expand your vocabulary, you will be able to read faster (in groups of words) because you don't have to take time to think what the words mean. Your brain has already processed it from memory. When you read more, you will encounter new words and you will learn more, thereby widening your vocabulary.

Practice Meta Guiding

Again, remember that the eyes have the habit of becoming fixated on objects that move. For instance, if you are sitting in front of the television, and a cockroach flies on your side, you will automatically focus on it. Or if you were talking to someone and a ball is suddenly thrown your way, you will naturally look towards it and react quickly. Eye fixation is a reflex that you should use to your advantage.

When you read, the words aren't moving but you can use your fingers or any kind of pointer so that your eyes will follow it. This is often referred to as meta guiding. It is an old technique that eliminates distractions and allows the reader to focus on important words so they can read faster.

Since the eyes are naturally attracted to movement, using a guide helps the reader expand their peripheral vision and be able to read multiple lines as guided. Using a guide helps control and improve eye fixations. It also gives the reader a way of navigating the layout and organization of the text, becoming more aware of headings and bolded texts, as well as looking for the ways in which the author transitions from one topic to the next.

As you use your guide, you can also regulate your speed so that you can go fast or slow as needed. Practice it and identify how much you can read in a minute. Keep on practicing and after a while, reading with the flow of your guide will come naturally and you will read smoothly.

Once you get better at speed reading, you can do away with your guide and your eyes will naturally move smoothly over the material.

You can read in increments in 1 to 5 minutes to track your progress. If you want to get an average of your speed rate (words per minute), count the number of lines you can read in a minute then multiply by ten – you use 10 because it is the average number of words per line in printed books. Every time you practice speed reading, make it a goal to beat your previous score. You will soon find yourself going faster.

Rapid Serial Visual Presentation

It has been established that when you make fewer eye fixations, you get to read and understand more words. When you master fixation, you will be able to master speed reading. In today's digital word, a digital method is also appropriate. Rapid Serial Visual Presentation or *RSVP* is helpful when you are reading material on a computer screen such as ebooks, online blogs and articles, and the like.

The RSVP is a speed reading system that allows the reader to focus on one word at a given time as it flashes on the screen. As you continue practicing this system, you will improve the speed with which you can read words on display then speed up the process.

For this, try **Spreeder** – it uses the latest innovations to make you more productive and efficient at speed reading. Go to https://www.spreeder.com/ to learn more. It is free.

Chapter 9: Comprehension Technique: Skimming+

Speed reading is more than just getting through a material very fast. It is about understanding the information you have just read better and quicker than you normally would. Speed reading is about efficiency.

Skimming is a skill that is often taught in grade school yet not developed as much. It allows the reader to scan through the content and detect important elements that are to be read. However, skimming does not make you a fast reader, although some people would say it is a speed reading technique.

This is because, as opposed to really reading, you merely scan and skip parts that you decide are not that essential. Usually, skimming allows for little comprehension and you don't always remember every word that you go through. Speed reading is skimming+, meaning it is more than just browsing or gliding through your text.

Skimming+ is all about getting the substance of what you are reading without having to read all the words. People use skimming as a speed reading technique when they have a lot of material to read and you don't have a lot of time to absorb it in detail. Keep in mind that skimming is three or four times faster than average reading so it means that your comprehension certainly declines in comparison.

If you really think about it, skimming is a lot like scavenging because you are looking for the choicest of information, hoping that you don't miss any important ones as you go along.

Skimming also allows you to get a general idea about the text. However, you need to know when you can skim a text and when you should read it in depth. When you choose skimming as your speed reading technique, you should know if the material is worth skimming.

You can skim lengthy business reports or white papers like annual reports or the newspaper. You can also skim through your book when you have an exam coming up and you don't have enough time to review. The key to knowing whether you should skim or not is to answer the following questions:

- *Do you have so much to read and not enough time?*
- *Is it non-fiction?*

- *Can you skip some of the material?*
- *Do you already have a background or familiar knowledge on the material?*

If your answers are yes to the questions, then you don't have to read everything and skimming can be helpful for you.

Here are some tips to properly skim through a material and recognize the essential information:

1. *Identify what your purpose is.*

Why are you reading what you are reading? When you know the reason, you will know what to look for. You will look out for and find terms that essentially express what it is you are looking for. When you don't know what you are looking for, you will skim without purpose which can be very boring and cause you to not retain many of the information you've just read.

2. *Read both ways – horizontally and vertically.*

Move your eyes up and down, and side to side. Imagine it as running down the stairs. You are trying to get down faster, but you are also being careful not to miss a step.

3. *Think like the writer.*

When you do so, you will skip out on unimportant details and just focus on the meat of the material. There is a point that the author is making, and as with number 1 – knowing what you want to get out of the material – you can detect what it is and gloss over examples and stories. It will take practice but you will learn the author's style – how he puts indirect information, secondary arguments and other tidbits.

4. *Find highlights or main ideas.*

Usually, the main idea is written in the beginning paragraphs of any material. Read it carefully so that you will understand the aim of the article. It is also important to read the first sentence of every paragraph. By doing so, you will know if it is worth reading fully and which ones you can skip.

Keep in mind that you don't have to go over the whole sentence if you find that is doesn't have any valuable information. You can skip through examples.

Chapter 10: Retention Technique: Maintain Focus

The world we live in offers so many distractions that it becomes hard to maintain focus while you are reading. Steve Jobs says that focus means you are saying no to the other ideas that are coming at you and picking the right one.

In essence, he is saying that focus is more than simply saying yes to one thing. If you do not try to cancel out the noise brought by the other ideas, you will not be able to concentrate on "the one". He stresses that innovation means you decline 1,000 other things.

Here are some simple tips and tricks that can help you keep and improve your concentration which will allow you to have better comprehension as you speed read.

1. *Turn of your notifications on email, instant messengers and mobile phone.*
You will always feel that you need to check your phone or computer for messages every time you hear that *ping!* go off. You don't have to. These nudges can take your attention away from what you are reading and when you lose concentration, you will find it hard to get back to speed reading.

You will find yourself having to re-read or you will lose interest entirely. Interruptions can also lower your brain's ability to concentrate on the information you are trying to hold. When you need to speed read, put your phone on silent mode and turn off all kinds of notifications. You can always check them after you read.

2. *Remember that proper posture is essential.*
Much like how it takes more muscles to frown than it does to smile, you need more energy to slouch that to sit properly. Make sure to practice proper posture when reading.
   - When sitting, push your hips far back to the chair. Your feet should be flat on the floor.
   - Your knees should be a bit lower or at the same height as your hips.
   - Get an ergonomic chair – your back should have proper support.

You will enjoy more benefits than just maintaining focus, you will stay healthy and avoid health issues that come with poor posture.

3. Clear your mind.

You only need a minute or two to do this. Regular meditation will help you a lot because it frees your mind from distractions and mental clutter. While you won't have enough time for proper meditation before you need to speed read a material, you can close your eyes for a minute or two, and release any stressful thoughts or cares that clutter your mind before you read. A relaxed mind will have a higher level of concentration.

4. Read in intervals.

A 50-minute interval is the most ideal time for focusing on an individual task, according to Peter Drucker. After fifty minutes, your mind will be tired and need a break. When you go beyond that mark, your mind becomes inefficient. You need to take a 10 minute break before you resume reading (or doing any task for that matter). Making this a habit will allow you to train your focus and use your brain at optimum levels.

5. Read with a purpose.

When you have a goal in mind, you will not read mindlessly. Reading with purpose will make going through the material easy and fast. When you have a specific goal set in your mind, you will concentrate better.

6. Find a good place to read.

Not only should you be in a comfortable, ergonomic seat, you should also be in a room where you won't be distracted by people who might constantly interrupt you. Likewise, eliminate unwanted noise as much as you can.

If you can read while music is being played, then play something easy to listen to. Most people find it not just relaxing to have a background music when doing something, it also helps them focus more. Of course it depends on the kind of music you are listening. Instrumental, classical music or even white noise will do wonders for your concentration.

7. *Make a mind map.*

It is important to work both sides of your brain in order to have better retention. The left side of your brain is for logic and structure while the right side is the artistic avenue. Engaging both while reading will help you retain more information and have better focus.

To train yourself to use both sides of your brain, make a mind map: take notes and draw images. You can first draw a picture of the topic you are reading or want/need to read, then add key words that are connected with it. Your brain will be using both sides as you do this.

When you do begin reading, your mind will just naturally come up with pictures and keywords and help you concentrate more and retain important information.

These are very simple tips but they are very useful and can create a big difference in your reading ability. Be sure to implement these regularly so you can get the benefits of maintaining your focus. You will also steadily improve your reading speed.

Chapter 11: Keys to Speed Reading Success

Whatever speed reading techniques you plan to apply, you must always be aware of the purpose of your reading and decide whether speed reading is the most appropriate approach.

When applied correctly and practiced diligently, speed reading can significantly improve your overall effectiveness, as it frees up precious time and allows you to work more efficiently in other areas.

<u>Keep the following in mind:</u>

1. Understanding *why* you should speed read is the start. When you know why you want to do something, it will be easy for you to implement the *how*.

2. Regular practice is essential – you need to make speed reading a habit. Any skill requires dedication and time. Do not be frustrated when it takes time to improve your speed reading skills.

3. You must break poor reading habits, as discussed in an earlier chapter. After you have done so, you will be able to develop and improve good speed reading skills. No matter how much you practice, poor reading habits can get in the way if you don't break them first.

4. Start your speed reading practice with easy material. If you start with something more challenging, you will most likely fail at it and become disappointed. Work your way up from short stories to a novel after you have practiced one-page or a couple of pages of easy-to-read documents until you become confident.

5. Remember that you cannot speed read everything. There are some things you need to read thoroughly in its entirety and give ample time to comprehend. These include letters from people you love, legal documents, important financial reports, novels, prose, information that needs to be memorized, and others of similar nature.

6. Learn how to benchmark your current reading speed. Benchmarking can help you monitor your progress. You can find speed reading assessments online.

7. Strengthen your eyes. Your eyes are your primary sense organ for reading so you should make them strong and ready for reading. This can be done through daily eye exercises and rest. The last chapter is dedicated to such exercises.

Chapter 12: Read a Book a Day - Speed Reading Exercises You Can Start and Make Into a Habit

Ultra-successful people like Warren Buffet, Bill Gates, John Maxwell, and Mark Zuckerberg believe in the power of reading books. Do you want to be able to read a book a day? As you begin to break bad reading habits that hold you back, you'll start to improve slowly but surely.

Here is a helpful guide to help you take that step:

1. **Wake up decisive.**

As soon as you wake up, smile and say, "Today is the day I will start learning the techniques for speed reading. And the next days are going to be awesome." Being positive and encouraging yourself will set your mind and focus into achieving your goal for the day: to speed read.

2. **Have a goal.**

You should decide how much to read every day. You don't have to finish one book in one sitting – but you will get there soon after much practice. For now, you can begin by practicing 10 minutes of speed reading one page a day. And you can increase that as you get the hang of speed reading – you will be able to read two pages in ten minutes the next day, three pages and so on.

You can also increase the amount of time you dedicate for your daily reading. It can be anything as long as you set a vision before you. Make sure to write smart, attainable goals, especially if you are in the beginning stages of making speed reading a habit. If you make big goals in the early stages of habit-forming, you may get discouraged early.

3. **Choose when to read.**

Choosing the time you sit down and get to reading is as important as choosing your material. The key is to know when you are at your optimal reading mood. Otherwise, you will struggle with distractions and feelings of tiredness and laziness.

You can read EARLY every day. Many students do this – they study early in the morning because the mind retains more information in the morning compared to when you stay up late into the night when the brain is tired.

When you wake up every day, do some reading even if it is only for 10 minutes. It will help enhance your concentration and you will be able to train your brain to improve your speed reading rate. *You can also choose to read BEFORE GOING TO BED.* Other people find that their minds are clearer and can be much more focused when they have attended to and completed their tasks for the day.

They can set aside worries and concerns for the next day, so this is the best time for them to read. Reading at night (especially if it's something enjoyable like fiction) is a proven way to relax.

But, of course, you can choose to read ANYTIME of the day. You can read a few pages after you finish lunch still have time before you have to get back to work. You can read during breaks at school. You can read while waiting for dinner to be cooked. You can read while having your afternoon tea.

The important thing: MAKE TIME. Don't out it off till tomorrow or the next day. Do it today.

4. **Get in the right environment.**

It will be quite difficult to read when you are not comfortable. With strained eyes and tired arms, neck or back, you will read at a slower pace, have lesser focus and understanding, and lose interest in reading altogether. Make sure that you get in the right reading environment by doing the following:

- Set up your reading space – one that is free from distractions.
- Get your tools ready: pen, paper, pointer, bookmark – whatever you need to use as a guide or for jotting down notes.
- Use a bookstand so that your reading angle is at 45 degrees.

- If you are going to read from a screen, it is better to use a tablet instead of reading from a desktop.
- Sit properly in a chair. Do not read in bed or while lying down.
- Make sure you have proper lighting.
- Allot at least one hour (50-minute straight reading, 10-minute rest) for reading and only to read and not do (or even think of) anything else.
- Play instrumental music or white noise using a headphone (optional).

5. Start Reading

Once you find the perfect reading atmosphere, you can go ahead and start reading. Keep in mind the different speed reading techniques you learned in the previous chapters. You can try one or try them all, but don't do it simultaneously. Choose what works for you.

6. Finish what you start.

Given that you started out with a goal, make sure that you are faithful to complete it. For example, if you decided to speed read for 50 minutes today, do not get up and close your book until that 50 minutes is up. It will take a good amount of self-discipline, but if you stick to fulfilling your goal for today, you will find it easier to do it in the succeeding days and you will form a good habit.

MAKE A COMMITMENT

Make a decision to do this for the next two weeks. Treat it as a "reading appointment" and faithfully attend to it. However, do not consider reading as an inconvenient routine like homework; instead, look at it like an experience that can change your perspective, enhance your imagination and improve other life skills.

Do not pressure yourself to finish one book in one day when you are just starting to build your speed reading skills. Initially, you can practice speed reading for 21 days – the amount of time it takes to form a habit – and follow the reading goal you set. You will build a great reading habit and you will soon find yourself someone who not just reads fast but also comprehends more – a speed reader!

Chapter 13: Speed Reading Tips that Enhance Your Habits

Good job on starting to speed read!

It will take time and effort and you may get discouraged along the way, but fear not – it is only the beginning and it will get better day by day. Here are some tips that can help you make that speed reading habit stronger:

1. **Use a timer.**

As you put to practice the speed reading techniques you have learned in this book, it is good to record your time and track your progress so you can increase your reading speed as you go along. Initially, you can set your timer to a minute, then read. When time is up, check the number of pages you have completed. You can get an app that will let you know how many words you read. Make a record your achievement.

Test your skill by doing the same exercise then see how much you have improved by comparing the results. You can set daily goals and start beating your own previous records. To stay motivate, reward yourself every time you beat a record. Turning it into an exciting game also means you won't notice how much effort you put into it and just enjoy the benefits! As you continue to practice the techniques everyday, you will get better.

2. **Use a marker.**

As you learned in chapter 7 and 8, reading fast without a guide can sometimes cause your vision to slip and slide. You may think that you have missed a word or failed to grasp something. There are many things you can use as a marker: your finger, a pen or pencil, a ruler, an index card or a bookmarker.

To use it, place the guide of your choice below every line that you read and glide it down as you continue. Using a marker will help you stay focused and ease your worry of not being able to take everything in. Here is a good exercise:

- For a minute, read a block of text at your regular pace but use a guide. Mark the place where you ended.

- For another minute, read starting from the beginning same text and try to get further than your first time, still using your guide.
- For the third time, read starting from the beginning of the same text and try to read three times farther in the same amount of time, one minute.
- After doing these, check yourself if you can remember what you have read or if you can piece the whole thought together. Go to the next portion and repeat the same practice.

This activity is designed to help you read faster so don't be pressured about recalling information. As you continue to practice this, you'll get better and better.

3. **Make yourself accountable.**

As with any goal, accountability helps to ensure that you are sticking to your methods of achieving your goal and keeps you on the right track. You can do it yourself by setting daily reading goals and having a checklist. Once you complete your daily reading requirement, tick it off your list.

You can also have someone check up on you. This doesn't mean that you should be hard on yourself. Give yourself an incentive when you meet a goal, and when you don't, encourage yourself to try harder the next time. Use accountability to motivate and inspire you.

4. **Use personal accountability techniques**

Dedicate a calendar for your speed reading goals. Hang it on the wall and mark each date with an X or a check mark as you complete your daily commitment. By doing so, you are putting a picture before you of your goal and your progress towards it.

As you see the satisfactory "did it" marks, you will have the motivation to not break your cycle – that is, to read every day. Set smart yet achievable goals to keep you both challenged and inspired to meet them.

5. **Improve your vocabulary.**

You can practice speed reading all you want but unless you widen your vocabulary, you will find it hard to have full comprehension of any material you read, and it will slow you down.

Often, you will encounter a word or set of words that you don't know. This will cause you to halt, or skip, or waste time thinking about what it actually means or if it is significant enough. You may find yourself stopping to ponder or look up its meaning. To avoid this, enhance your vocabulary. The more words you know, the easier it will be for you to speed read and you will be able to read and know a whole lot more.

6.   Ask questions.

You can boost your reading comprehension by checking through headings and subtitles and turning them into questions. This will help you understand what you are looking for when you scan through the text. This is also a good way to increase your reading speed and enhance your focus.

When you know what you are looking for – answers to the questions you formed – you will be more focused and alert to what you are reading.

7.   Preview and jot down brief notes.

Just like how movies would have a preview, you can get a glimpse of the content of what you are about to read by doing a preview. First, look over the material and find out what is important and interesting. You will also know which ones to skip so that you can focus on what you need to remember.

This will save you time and effort. You can enhance your reading speed and steer clear of re-reading by writing down notes, or making an outline, after reading something. You can use these notes as reference when you need to make a response or a course of action.

8.   Do not highlight.

A lot of people use highlighters in order for them to remember important text, thinking it improves their comprehension. It is not true. When you highlight something, you are training your mind to focus on the text that is highlighted, instead of learning the whole material. The problem with this is you may have to re-read the whole thing again since you didn't fully comprehend it to start with.

It's better to speed read – read and understand fully – than to just highlight facts that you deem necessary. There may be information that you have to know that you failed to highlight.

9.   Always bring your book with you.

As part of your daily routine, bring your current read along with you so that you can catch up on your reading whenever you find the opportunity; like an unexpected long lunch-hour line at your favourite restaurant or waiting in the bus or subway.

10.   Prepare your next book.

Even if you are not yet done with the first one, you can go to the bookstore and choose the new book you are going to read next. When you do this, you are preventing yourself from being stuck without a reading material and feeling sluggish about continuing with your practice. It is better if you can come up with a line-up of books to read for the month.

11.   Decide to read, read, read.

Practice always makes perfect. It is true with any skill you wish to learn. Read more and you will become better at it. You can read average-length documents, books, papers, pamphlets, newspapers – anything. Just do it often. This will fuel your goal of improving your rate of reading.

It is also important to remember that you don't have to put pressure on yourself to read what others are reading. Reading should be for your own enjoyment, pleasure, and education. Just because it's the current bestseller doesn't mean you have to get your hands on it because if it is a topic that you won't find exciting, you will just lose interest.

12.   Learn to stop.

While it is a good goal to finish what you start, you don't have to apply this to every book that you read. Do not feel pressured-- as if you will receive punishment for partially reading a book.

If it's something you don't enjoy, you can close the book and pick up another one. Don't feel bad about it and don't let it become an obsession. As a popular saying goes, "life is too short to read lousy books". More importantly, when your eyes are tired, stop. Do not overexert your eyes or you might suffer injury.

13.   Prioritize reading.

Often you think that you have so much to do, but have very little time in your hands. But if you make reading a priority, you will soon find yourself having extra time to do other things.

To help you prioritize, you can organize your reading materials into three categories: important, average, and least important. Make sure that you read according to importance. As you read the more important materials first, you will have better focus. Not only will you improve your speed, you will also give more time and attention to things that matter most.

14.   Borrow or purchase more books than you can read.

When you are surrounded by books, you will have easy access to reading. When you find a good book in the store, get it. When you borrow books from the library and put them in a pile at home, you will be motivated to read them as you have to return them at a certain date. Having books at home also ensures that you have easily available choices when you do need some reading material.

15.   Always do eye exercises.

In the next chapter, you will learn about different eye exercises you can do on a daily basis to strengthen your eye muscles. Eye movement is very crucial in speed reading and when you build your eye muscles, the faster you will read and you will avoid eye strain.

When you make time to practice regularly, you will become a more efficient speed reader. This discipline can even overflow into different areas of your life – you will find yourself learning new things fast and grasping new concepts easily. Don't worry, you can always control your speed! You don't have to feel pressured to speed read all the time.

Chapter 14: Eye Exercises for Speed Reading

Speed reading involves a lot of eye movement. The muscles around your eyes can be strengthened so that you won't strain your eyes whenever you speed read. Exercise will also give you more flexibility and clearer vision. Strong eye muscles will also deteriorate less with aging. Here are some daily eye exercises you can do to make those muscles strong.

1. **Thumb glancing**

This exercise will stretch the muscles in your eye sockets to make them more flexible and strengthen your peripheral vision as well.

- Sit or stand up.
- Stretch both of your arms to the sides. Your thumbs should be sticking up.
- Look straight ahead for a few seconds, then slowly move your eyes to glance at your left thumb.
- Then use your eyes to glance at your right thumb.
- Do not move your head while you are doing this exercise, just your eyes.
- Glance back and forth ten times.
- Repeat the whole activity three times.

2. **Resting eyes**

This is a good way to relax your eyes, especially when it needs to rest.

- Shut your eyes halfway and do your best not to let them quiver.
- While it is half-closed, look towards a faraway object. You will feel that there will be less to no trembling as you gaze.
- Do this activity two to three times.

3. **Eye-writing**

When you write with your eyes, you are forcing it to move out of its normal fashion, giving you more flexibility. This workout will strengthen the ocular muscles in your eye sockets and give you better range of motion.

Accelerated Learning

- Sit or stand up.
- Look at the wall that is on the farthest line of sight from where you are sitting or standing.
- Picture in your mind that you are writing your name or any word on the wall using your eyes.
- Use your eyes to write your name or any word. Do not move your head along. Only your eyes should be moving like a pen or paintbrush as you "write".
- Write in capital letters.
- Write in small letters.
- Write in cursive.

4. **Eye squeeze**

These squeezes that involve breathing exercises can help relax your eyes and increase the oxygen and blood flow to the face and around the eyes.

- Open your eyes and mouth wide, stretching your facial muscles, and inhale deeply.
- As you exhale, close your eyes, clench your jaws and squeeze your facial muscles, as well as the muscles in your head and neck, very tightly.
- Hold your breath for the next thirty seconds and continue squeezing.
- Repeat the steps 4 times.
- Take a short 1-minute break
- Do another round of eye squeezes.
- Do this five times.

Conclusion

Thank you again for purchasing this book!

I hope this book was able to help you better understand how you can use speed reading to your advantage: read faster, comprehend better, learn more, and be an expert at retaining information.

You have learned the different speed reading techniques and how you can apply them in your daily life.

The next step is to start doing the exercises you learned from this book, ones which will help you create a habit of speed reading. Take that first step and begin speed reading today.

Forget about your initial misconceptions about speed reading and begin to read more efficiently. No matter what level of speed reading you are now, there is always room for improvement. It may take a lot of work in the beginning but remember that you cannot have something significant if you don't put in a significant amount of work into it.

Put your heart into it – excellence is at your fingertips!

Book – II
Photographic Memory

Simple, Proven Methods to Remembering Anything Faster, Longer, Better

Introduction

If I tell you to imagine 9,471,037,094,871 wolves flying in the sky, you'll probably picture a pack of flying wolves in your head; but will you imagine the exact number of wolves? No, you won't—bet you didn't even bother reading the numbers, did you?

Our minds find it easier to process information that has a picture of an existing object than something that is purely abstract. That is why people can remember faces more quickly than telephone numbers. After imagining the case above, you probably can still remember what kind of animals you have just imagined. However, if you will be asked, "how many wolves were there in your imagination?" You'll probably need to go back to the first paragraph before you can answer.

The reason behind such is that our minds can visualize words but not numbers. Visualization is the process of forming mental images in mind. These mental images stay in the mind longer than plain text and numbers. People associate this with the term "photographic memory." It is said to be the ability to remember a memory depicting a scene or a picture, and being able to mentally examine every detail on it.

There are a lot of things, however, beyond the term "photographic memory" that you need to know. Things about your mind that can help you clearly understand how your memory works. Things that can be the key to achieve an extraordinary retention capacity. Your memory has a lot of secrets and tricks—it's just waiting for you to discover them firsthand.

Chapter 1: Understanding the Memory

Memory is one of the key mental faculties. It is the mind's ability to retain and retrieve information. To understand how information is processed to become a memory, it is important to know the three main stages of memory creation: encoding, storage, and retrieval.

Encoding happens when the brain registers the stimulus that the body receives through its senses. A stimulus is basically anything that triggers the body to react or respond. Once it reaches the brain, the brain will decide whether to delete it or encode it. Attention plays an important role in this process as it determines whether the new information is going to be encoded or not. The more attention a stimulus receives, the more likely it is going to be encoded.

The storage phase is the actual process of retention. This is where the information is filtered into either short-term or long-term memory. Emotions highly influence the storage process as information with an elevated degree of emotional impact tend to be stored more in the long-term memory. The retrieval stage, on the other hand, is the process through which the mind recalls the previously stored information. It is what makes a memory an actual memory for it is where "remembering" happens.

One of the models that have greatly influenced the study of memory is the Atkinson–Shiffrin memory model, proposed by Richard Atkinson, a professor of psychology; and Richard Shiffrin, a professor of cognitive science on 1968. According to this model, a human memory is composed of three components namely, sensory register, short-term memory, and long-term memory.

Sensory Register

A sensory register—a register or stimulus received through the senses—usually does not reach the storage phase as it is easily forgotten or neglected. According to Akinson and Shiffin, the mind is prevented from receiving an overwhelming number of stimuli because a sensory register decays immediately unless it receives enough amount of attention. If it does, the brain stores it in the short-term memory.

Short-term Memory

A short-term memory, also known as a working memory, is a memory that can stay in the brain for about 18 to 30 seconds if not rehearsed. Akinson and Shiffin explained that an information is rehearsed when it is repeated over and over in one's brain. A short-term memory can further be transferred into the long-term storage of memories.

Long-term Memory

When an information is held in the short-term memory storage for a considerably long period, it is automatically transferred to the long-term memory storage; thus, it becomes a long-term memory. Traumatic and other experiences that have impacted a person emotionally are usually brought to the long-term memory store. The period of time within which a long-term memory is stored is indefinite. It can last for a year or for a lifetime and is usually lost only when the brain starts deteriorating, itself.

Chapter 2: Photographic Memory

Photographic memory is associated with the visual memory system of the brain. The mental images your brain receives through your vision of any object, is stored to the visual memory. It is also where your brain can retrieve information in the form of an image. The type of sensory register that brings visual stimulus or "icon" to the brain is called the iconic memory.

Instances like being able to visualize where exactly that answer in an exam is located on the book, or being able to imagine the sequence of all the things on a list, is commonly attributed to photographic memory. The term "photographic memory" is generally used interchangeably with the term "eidetic memory."

Eidetic Memory

Although both terms are used interchangeably, eidetic memory is not completely the same with photographic memory. Eidetic memory is the ability to recall memories in the form of images or "photographs". The visuals created under eidetic memory is vivid and accurately detailed; although there are factors which can alter it as any memory is subject to distortion. Additionally, the image is usually gone in just a matter of seconds or minutes, after the icon fades or upon interference of an action such as blinking.

So how is it different from photographic memory? Photographic memory, in contrast to eidetic memory, is the ability to recall information in a very detailed manner. It is said that if a person has a photographic memory, he can remember the exact numbers or text on a page as if the actual page is in front of the eyes.

Another thing is that photographic memory is said to be limited only to the visual memory. Eidetic memory, on the other hand, involves other senses like auditory, olfactory, and tactile. Furthermore, eidetic imagery capability has only been found in children and not in adults.

Setting Your Mind

"But I don't have a photographic memory?"

As defined above, the term "photographic memory" really seems to be an ability that is impossible to attain. It sounds like a talent that can be acquired only when you're born with it and not a skill that you can learn. Actually, there is no solid scientific evidence to this "photographic memory" that exists today. But come to think of it, what if we redefine the term "photographic memory?"

You may be starting to wonder, "how can those people with extraordinary memories remember information if they do not have a photographic memory?" Answers to that question may vary but let me emphasize the most realistic answer of all—skills.

Those people rely purely on their skills to memorize patterns and details among sets of information; thus, you call them skilled and not necessarily talented. These skills are what makes them look like they have a photographic memory. If we try to link these skills and techniques to the term "photographic memory," we can actually derive a more realistic definition for the same exact term.

Believe me, the concept of photographic memory is so near to the concepts of the most renowned memorization techniques today. These techniques have been making dramatic improvements among people's memory for centuries. And you know what makes these techniques better? It is the fact that you are about to learn these skills as you read more through the chapters. So, let us start redefining the photographic memory, and most importantly—start redefining how your own memory works.

Chapter 3: Creative Thinking

The idea of photographic memory and the techniques that you will eventually learn are both under the same concept—creative thinking. Creative thinking is your way to meet the demands of a great memory; but what exactly is creative thinking?

Imagine you are in a zoo along with some tourists, and the tour guide introduces the following animals to you:

- Lark the zebra
- Cupid the tiger
- Red the elephant
- Nick the giraffe
- King the lion
- Orange the gorilla
- Lizzie the python
- Kurt the hippopotamus
- Bryce the ostrich

Now that they have just been introduced to you, can you recite all of their names without looking back on the list?

If you tried to but couldn't recite all of them, then it is most probably either because you just read their names or because you just said their names out loud – perhaps twice, as you think that is how your memory works. Well, it is true that repetition of an idea increases the chances of it, being retained inside your head; but the main problem with that practice is, you cannot jump into the exact position of an idea without reciting the whole list over again.

Let's say for example, without looking at the list, can you tell the name of the hippopotamus? You cannot remember it immediately, can you? Memorizing a list plainly is basically memorizing a sequence. The issue with it is that your mind needs to stick to the order of data in order to retrieve memories properly. Meaning, you cannot jump into a particular information without first reciting some or all of the information that come before it. This is where creativity needs to enter.

Creativity expands the encoding capacity of the brain. It makes the stimuli reach the storage phase by somehow forcing them to undergo an unconventional way of encoding. As you have learned in one of the previous chapters, a datum is only encoded in the brain when it is given attention otherwise it is going to decay instantly. Once encoded, the level of attention provided will dictate whether the datum is going to be stored or not. Creative methods of memorization boost the attention level that the brain can normally provide to a certain stimulus. There are a lot of basic ways you can learn to provide a solid foundation to your creative thinking but in here, we'll focus only on the three Cs: clueing, connecting, and creating.

Clueing

Let's forget about the list of those adorable animals for a while and discuss about the first C which is the clueing. If you are memorizing names, try to find something along the letters in the subject's name that you think resembles or gives a "clue" about the subject, itself. Let's take Nick the giraffe as an example. What do all giraffes have in common? A super long neck. Now, if you are going to analyze, Nick is just one letter different from the word "neck." In this case, you have found a clue that will make you interpret Nick as neck and eventually link it to the giraffe you have just met in the zoo.

You can also use the clueing method to Lark the zebra and Kurt the hippopotamus. If you are going to replace the L with an M, Lark will turn into mark. And what distinguishes zebras from other horses? It's the presence of stripes on their skin. They have "mark"s on them. So, the zebra with marks is named Lark. On the other hand, Kurt the hippopotamus lives in the dirt. Or you can say that Kurt lives in the dirt. "Kurt" rhymes with "dirt." Therefore, if you need to remember what the hippopotamus' name is, just remember he lives in the dirt.

Connecting

The second C requires an extended and somehow, more logical reasoning. Let's use King the lion as an example. King is actually the easiest to remember since lions are labeled as kings of the jungle. But even without the term "king of the jungle," you can still easily connect the name "King" to a lion. A king is always looked up as a man of pride and coincidentally, a group of lions is called a pride. Lion is to pride, and pride is to a king; hence, the lion is King.

Lizzie, on the other hand, sounds almost like lazy. Just imagine that the python was so lazy that all it ever does is crawl the whole day and voila! You'll now be able to remember who's the Lizzie-est (laziest) of them all! The gorilla named Orange seems like hard to remember but using the connecting method, you can tie up the subject with its name. The word that will serve as a link to connect "Orange" to "gorilla," is the "orangutan." Replacing the "-utan" in orangutan with a letter E, you can get the word "Orange." Think of it as if "Orange" is a name for an orangutan. But since there was no orangutan in the zoo, the nearest alternative you'd think of is an animal that belongs to the same species—in your case, the gorilla.

Creating, the third C, will be elaborately discussed on the next chapter. It is the most flexible method which can be used to effectively encode whatever data or information you want your mind to store. Since you have learned about the first two methods, it will be easier for you to understand the idea of creating mental images or visualization. Onto the next chapter!

Chapter 4: Visualization

Unlike the first two methods of basic creative thinking, creating is not limited to connecting or finding a clue using the letters of the word. In fact, it does not have any limit at all. And the best thing about creating is that it does not follow formality and propriety. It doesn't even have to be realistic and logical. As long as you use your imagination, you are basically free to use this method.

The term "creating" refers to the projection or creation of a mental image in the mind by the use of imagination. For this reason, we can also call this method "visualization" which is the common term for such process. There is only one rule you need to follow when you are visualizing or creating—exaggerate.

Let's start with Cupid the tiger. Cupid does not have a general connection with the animal tiger. In this case, the only option you have is to create a visual inside your head that will make you remember "Cupid" as the name of the tiger in that zoo. So, I need you to imagine a pink-colored tiger whose fur, instead of striped, is marked with tiny red heart-shaped spots. Imagine it always flies around the forest using the pair of white feather wings on its back. It's like the famous Cupid of Valentine's Day but the difference is that it is a tiger and not a child.

The next example we have is Red the Elephant. Sure, the word "red" is so easy to remember; but can you still remember it when it is mixed with the other names? To attach the word "red" to elephant, think of a red-colored elephant that is as tiny as an ant. An elephant that is the size of an ant doesn't exist but your mind will remember it, as well as its color and name. What's the rule again? Exaggerate. If your mind can enlarge something to a size of a planet, then it can also reduce the size of something down to an atom.

For the last example, we have Bryce the ostrich. Ostrich is known to be one of those birds which cannot fly due to the unbalanced proportion between their puny wings and their heavy body weight. Imagine the utter disappointment the ostrich in that zoo felt when he found out that he couldn't fly despite being a bird. Every time he sees other birds fly, he feels so frustrated that he cries. Using the rhyming method, if an ostrich cries, then its name is Bryce.

How Visualization Sticks to the Memory

You already know that it is the attention which decides whether a stimulus is going to be encoded or not. If you are strolling around a park and you see a couple, you will probably forget about them minutes after; but if you come across a cosplayer, you'll probably spend few seconds longer looking at the details of his costume. It is more probable that you'll remember the cosplayer rather than the couple. Attention is relatively high when the brain receives uncommon stimuli. Therefore, when the body senses something strange, the stimuli immediately pass through the encoding stage and subsequently enter the storage process, even in the absence of consciousness.

Same thing happens when the brain creates mental image on its own. Visualization of a scenario that happens on a day to day basis like eating, taking a bath, and sleeping, is not necessarily retained in your memory because your mind does not generally attend to such things. But imagining impossible happenings like eating a chocolate cake that is as huge as your house, or sleeping on a bed that floats above the sea by itself, usually causes the brain to pay attention and consider encoding the stimuli.

Mental images that are unrealistic and exaggerated stick more to the memory because their oddity is easier to remember. When you retrieve a memory, your brain readies all the available pictures that can specifically satisfy what you want to remember. However, if there are a lot of pictures that look similar to what you want to remember, chances are you will get an altered or distorted memory. Similarity among memories can cause alteration of the real scene and might cause the memories to overlap. Differently, when something odd is encoded in the brain, there is no other comparable material that can cause conflict during retrieval; hence, the visual representation of the memory is more precise and is more easily remembered. Visualization might be weird and all but remember, what is out of this world is usually what stays in your mind.

Now let's go back to the list of the animals introduced by the tour guide but this time you need to fill in the blanks using your memory. See if you can remember them all:

- _____ is the name of the elephant
- Lizzie is a _____
- Orange is a _____
- _____ is the hippopotamus
- Cupid is a _____ while King is a _____
- _____ is the name of the ostrich
- The zebra's name is _____
- Nick is a _____

"Visualization takes much effort. How is it better than the method of repeating information?" Repeating the set of information over and over until retained might seem to be easier at first. But is only because you are used to memorizing things that way. You haven't tried visualization much so you think it would take more time and effort for you to imagine a scenario for every separate information. But if you use this method more frequently, you'll find out that it's actually easy. Plus, it trains your brain to be more resourceful with the available knowledge you have. It will take a lot of practice but hey, practice is the only key to an ultimate memory anyway.

Chapter 5: Introduction to Memorization Techniques

From now on, the basics of creative thinking will serve as your foundation to everything that you are going to learn. So, it would be best to make sure that you fully understand them. Although you don't have to worry about not yet being able to master them as you don't have to. Creative thinking takes a lot of practice and experience; therefore, so is advanced memorization techniques.

During the old ages, people did not have access to instant memorization aids. Writing a long script would just consume a large amount of ink. Cue cards were not yet widely used. Besides, assistance is not quite good for the image of any orator or speaker that time. There were no visual aids, no PowerPoint, and no other materials that would help them remember information better and faster. Thus, memorization was all about pure skill.

In order to remember massive information, people created several techniques that would help their brain retain multiple sets of data without the need of aiding materials. These people are also called "mnemonists" which is the term for individuals who possess exceptional ability to recall a number of details with ease. Since then, the invented techniques have been proven to provide dramatic results. In fact, majority of them are still being used today.

Rote Learning

Rote learning is the usual yet least favored technique of knowledge retention. It is similar to Akinson and Shiffrin's rehearsal wherein a person repeats a list of information over and over until retained in his memory. It is the least favored technique because it tends to skip the actual learning process and does not promote creativity. Unless rehearsed more frequent than usual, information encoded through rote learning usually does not last more than a day since it already starts fading in just a matter of hours. This is the reason it is used by students who cram or who memorize lessons few hours before their actual exam.

Mnemonics

Another usual technique used most especially in school is the mnemonic. This is normally used to memorize details that belong to a common group or list. Instead of memorizing the whole list, the initials or parts of the words are combined to form another word, phrase, or sentence which is easier to remember.

Linking

Rote learning and mnemonics may not require visualization; but linking, together with all the other proceeding techniques, requires one. Linking is the method of connecting adjacent details on a list. It's basically visualizing mental images that represent the connection of the first detail to the second one, the second detail to the third one, the third detail to the fourth one, and so on. To demonstrate, take note of the given short list of the first world countries below:

- United States
- Canada
- Bermuda
- Iceland
- Denmark
- Switzerland
- Ireland

- San Marino
- Norway
- Luxembourg

Using the linking method, you need to choose a visual for each of the country listed. You may start the sequence of scenarios with a picture of yourself, watching shooting stars (America's star-spangled flag) in slow motion. Next, imagine the stars that hit the ground eventually transforming into maple leaves (Canada's maple leaf). After then, the maple leaves started turning green as if they are creating a field of bermudagrass (Bermuda). Then the bermudagrass field started turning into an ice field (Iceland), and so on and so forth. Again, exaggerate the scenarios. They do not have to be realistic. And that's how simple the linking method goes. It is a good option when you want remember a list of data that follows a strict order.

Peg Systems

Peg systems are also good for data in sequence. They are one of the most effective memorization techniques as a single peg can be applied to different lists. It initially requires a preliminary list before the memorizing the actual information needed. You will learn more about the pegs in the next chapter.

Emotion-based Memorization

One of the aspect that affects the storage of an information is the emotional content. In this technique, an individual applies emotion to each information on the list. The emotion to associate with each detail should, as much as possible, be distinct from that of the other. This technique requires a deeper connection to imagination since emotions during visualization should be felt by the user as if they are real. This will be further explained on chapter 7.

Mind Map

Mind map or mind mapping is the use of a diagram to mentally organize information in mind. This method is fit for those individuals who can maintain focus while creating a detailed diagram inside their head; although the diagram can also be initially drawn on a piece of paper. Mind mapping is commonly used to memorize a whole set of related information such a lesson with topics and subtopics. This technique will be elaborated on chapter 8.

Visualizing Names

People often find issues when it comes to memorizing names. Fortunately, there is a certain technique that is developed to make remembering names easier. You'll learn about this technique on chapter 9.

Visualizing Numbers

Methods under this suggest a way to ease the difficulties on memorizing numbers. They are actually one of those peg systems but they are specifically developed to deal with numbers. They use representations to help the mind visualize numbers. The specific techniques will be demonstrated on chapters 10 and 11.

Memory Palace

Mnemonists label this technique as the most effective method of memorization. It is pretty much like creating a storage inside your head in the form of any physical object through which you can consciously retrieve information with ease. The size and complexity of the storage depends on your choice. You can make the memory storage look as simple as a cabinet or as complex as a maze. You'll find out how it works and how easy it is to learn on chapter 12.

Chapter 6: Peg Systems

Peg systems are a type of memorization technique wherein an individual memorizes an initial or original list of representational objects that will later be used to memorize another list of information. The objects on the initial list serve as the "pegs" of the system and each of them represents and substitutes a certain number. Thus, instead of memorizing the information by their numerical sequence, you can just assign a peg to each of them.

The initial list generally does not change and does not contain the actual information to memorize. It is like a permanent list in your mind that is meant to be associated with any other list of information and is usually made of easy-to-visualize words. This technique is commonly used to memorize a sequence of information.

There are different types of peg systems namely, the number rhyme, the number shape, the alphabet system, the major system, and the PAO system. Although similar in purpose, each of them has a different way of assigning pegs to a number of information.

Number Rhyme

From the name itself, the number rhyme uses the names of objects that rhyme with the numbers on the list. To further understand, take a look at the list below and try to memorize it:

01 - bun (as in bread roll)

02 - shoe

03 - tree

04 - boar

05 - hive (as in beehive)

06 - cheeks

07 - heaven

08 - plate

09 - sign (as in street signs)

10 - hen (as in a female bird)

The list is what we call an original list. Once pre-memorized, it can be associated with another list that contains the information you need to memorize. You may choose to assign your own pegs or just adopt the same list. It's completely up to you. Just make sure that your mind can easily picture each word since you don't want your original list to be an additional burden. But for this specific exercise, we will be using the mentioned list.

Let's say for example, you need to shop groceries but for a certain reason, you do not want to bring a grocery list. So, in order to make sure that you will not miss any item, you decided to memorize the list before going to the supermarket.

Grocery List:

- shampoo
- toothpaste
- soda in can
- apple juice
- lemons
- prunes

- tomatoes

- beef

- bell pepper

- cabbage

Now, try to associate your grocery list to the original list you have using the number rhyme peg system. The first thing on your to-buy list is shampoo while the first word on your initial list is bun. So, imagine yourself eating a bun with a shampoo filling. Yes, it's gross but remember, that is how things stick in your mind. Moving on, try to imagine yourself cleaning your white shoes with toothpaste. That shall connect "shoe" with "toothpaste." Next, think of a tree that bears sodas in can as its fruits so you can quickly remember the not-so-healthy third item. Following the rest of the list, imagine the following scenarios in sequence: a boar swimming in a pond of apple juice, a beehive that contains lemons instead of honey, your cheeks getting so wrinkled that they start looking like prunes, angels in heaven throwing tomatoes at each other while playing, a huge plate containing a meat of beef that is as large as the table, a green traffic sign in the shape of a bell pepper, and a hen sitting on her nest that is made of cabbage leaves.

You can use the original list you developed over and over again to memorize another set or list of information. That is how the number rhyme system—and generally the peg systems—is used. You don't have to force your brain to enumerate all the items on your grocery list. You just need to reimagine all the scenarios you have made in your head using the peg system.

Number Shape

01 - pen

02 - swan

03 - flying bird

04 - flag

05 – hook hand or hook

06 - golf club

07 - ramp

08 - infinity sign

09 - balloon

10 - snail

To explain how each peg is related to its corresponding number, imagine these numbers forming the shapes of the pegs. The number one is like a pen. Number two is like the curve from a swan's breast up to its bill. Three is that m-shaped bird we all have drawn when we were young. Four is like a flag with a triangular banner. Five is like a pirate's hook hand facing down. Six's shape is like a golf club. Seven is like a skateboard ramp rotated 90°. Eight is just a vertical infinity sign. Nine is like a balloon. Ten is like a snail crawling up a rock or a snail rotated 90°; its body is the number one while its shell is the zero.

Unlike number rhyme, the number shape uses the shape of the objects to substitute numbering. Again, you can change the images if you have a better replacement or something that is easier for you to imagine. Of course, you have to memorize the images first before you can memorize the information you need. Let us use the same grocery list which was cited previously on the number rhyme system as an example.

First, imagine yourself writing on a paper using a pen which uses shampoo as its ink. Second, imagine a swan living on a lake that is made up of toothpaste instead of water. Third, imagine a flying bird drinking soda in the sky. Fourth, think of a large apple with a flag on top. Fifth, imagine yourself as a pirate captain eating a lemon with your hook hand. Sixth, picture yourself playing golf and hitting prunes that are as large as golf balls. Seventh, imagine you are a skateboarder and one of your exhibitions is skating up a ramp while juggling tomatoes. Eighth, visualize your refrigerator producing infinite number of beef every day. Ninth, imagine a bell pepper floating like a balloon up the sky. Tenth, imagine a gigantic snail whose shell is an actual cabbage.

Alphabet Peg System

If you prefer organizing the information using the letters in the English alphabet system instead of numbering them, then you can use the alphabet peg system. It works basically the same way as the previous peg systems except that you associate information with pegs that represent the letters in the alphabet. It also can only cover up to 26 pieces of information due to the limited characters of the alphabet.

There are three methods under the alphabet peg system namely, the initial letter method, the letter sound method, and the letter shape method. The original list created under the initial letter method contains objects whose names start with the corresponding letters in the alphabet. For example: axe, ball, carpet, door, egg, fork, gun, house, etc.

The letter sound method, on the other hand, uses objects whose sounds start the same as the sounds of the letters in the alphabet like "ape" for a, "bin" for b, "sea" for c, etc. The letter shape, of course, uses objects whose shapes are almost like those of the letters; so, you can imagine a ladder for A, eyeglasses rotated 90° for B, or a crescent moon for C.

Let's say for example you have to memorize the 17 basic types of psychology for an exam. Using the initial letter method, you've come up with the list below:

A - axe

B - barber

C - chicken

D - dog

E - egg

F - fireworks

G - gate

H - house

I - ink

J - juice

K - knife

L - leaf

M - moon

N - necklace

O - oven

P – phone

Q - queen

To start, imagine a man whirling his axe on the street scaring people (abnormal psychology). Then think of a barber who keeps on insulting his customers. People say his attitude is in his genes (behavioral genetics). The chicken in your neighborhood is actually a biological child of your neighbors (biological psychology); it's their son. Imagine a smart dog that talks about problem solving skills (cognitive psychology). Visualize an egg singing a European song while being boiled in its Asian-themed shell (cross-cultural psychology). Imagine the fireworks spelling out "I'm different" in the sky (differential psychology). Think of an old-looking gate that serves as a portal to a hidden cultural museum (cultural psychology). Think of a house that is under development (developmental psychology). Think of the word "evolution" written in ink (evolutionary psychology). Imagine experimenting with the different flavors of juice (experimental psychology). Imagine yourself stabbing your Math test paper with a knife because you can't answer the problems (mathematical psychology). Imagine discovering a kind of leaf that improves the functions of all your neurons (neuropsychology). Imagine the moon telling you how he likes the sun's personality (personality psychology). Visualize yourself wearing a necklace with a plus pendant (positive psychology). Think of an oven that bakes numbers (quantitative psychology). Try to compare your new phone with the first phone you had (comparative psychology). Imagine a queen who keeps on hanging out with her friends and acquaintances (social psychology).

Now try to answer the following questions without looking back to the mentioned types of psychology above:

- What type of psychology is linked to the barber who insults his customers?
- What type of psychology is associated with the chicken in your neighborhood?
- What type of psychology does the boiled egg represent?
- What type of psychology is linked to the hidden gate?
- What type of psychology does the knife represent?
- What type of psychology is associated with the necklace with a plus pendant?
- What type of psychology is linked to the queen who always hangs out with her friends?

If you answered at least four questions right, then that means you are doing great. However, if you were not able to attain four correct answers, that's fine. You can still learn and practice more techniques as you go further through the next chapters, including the other peg systems that have special and specific purposes.

Chapter 7: Emotion-based Memorization

Can you still recall the first lesson you had in high school? Well, there's actually a high possibility that you can't. But, do you still remember your first heart break? Of course, you do. No matter how painful, saddening, or fulfilling it was, nobody forgets his first love.

Actually, the fact that your first heart break was painful, saddening, or fulfilling, is the exact reason you still remember it. Information that is charged with enough level of any emotion is more likely to be encoded and stored. As previously mentioned, emotions play an important role in the encoding phase for it heightens the level of attention designated to a certain stimulus. This means that emotions serve as a guarantee for a certain stimulus to subconsciously pass through encoding process; thus, greater probability of getting stored in the brain.

Moreover, emotions can dominate the importance of information. Long-term memory store contains more emotionally-driven memories than consciously injected information. If I tell you to remember any happy moment there will surely be one that is going to pop up in your head. But if I tell you to recite your company's or school's contact number, you won't recall it quickly or possibly, you won't recall anything at all because you simply do not have a memory of it stored in your brain. Your happy moments cannot save you in case of emergency but the school's or company's contact number can. However, your brain tends to easily retrieve those moments quickly as they are charged with feelings—happiness—unlike the contact number which needs to be rehearsed multiple times despite its importance to you.

Mood

An emotional aspect that is closely related to the functioning of memory is the mood. It is a less specific emotional state brought not necessarily by external stimuli but by internal factors. The surroundings and external events, which are considered external factors, may also influence a certain person's mood although the mood, itself is initiated by one's own mind state.

Mood affects a person's memory in two ways: mood congruence and mood dependence. Mood congruence happens when you remember memories that depict the mood you are currently feeling. For example, if you feel like you are in a bad mood, or more specifically feeling irritable at the moment, there is a possibility that you will be able to remember an event from the past where you also felt extremely annoyed by anyone or anything. This is what mood congruence means. The mood of the memory you retrieve is similar to the mood you are feeling during retrieval.

Mood dependence, on the other hand, affects both the encoding and retrieval phases. It suggests that recalling an event is easier when it was encoded under the same mood that you are currently having during retrieval. For example, when an information from the past was encoded in your brain during a happy moment, it will be easier to remember it when you are also feeling happy while retrieving it. The mood you had when you were encoding a memory is the same as the mood you are feeling during retrieval. To further clarify the subtle differences between the two effects, under the mood congruence, the mood during retrieval matches the mood of the memory, itself regardless how you were feeling while your brain was encoding it; while under the mood dependence, the mood during retrieval matches the mood during encoding regardless of the mood the memory being encoded is depicting.

Applying Emotions to Visuals

If only every information had emotional content attached to it, then you would be able to remember memories effortlessly. Sadly, things do not work that way. Extreme emotions are brought by reality and those emotionally-charged memories that stick forever to you only come from actual events. For you to remember the moments when you were still in love with someone, you have to experience the real feeling of "love" otherwise the mind will consider it as a temporary thought.

But come to think of it, there are a number of information that you need to retain not necessarily for a lifetime; but only for a rather lengthy period so you can store them in your mind at least until you actually use them. This just means you do not need to attain the realistic peaks of emotions. You just have to feel something less intense than reality but more realistic than imagination.

If the thoughts of hearing fingernails scrape a chalkboard gives you shiver, then you are more or less capable of feeling illusory emotions. You are going to need this ability to enhance your retention along with your visualization skill. Also, in applying emotions, remember that you need to be honest as much as possible. Focus on the realistic feeling you would get if the same thoughts happened in reality.

Let's start with a familiar example: Bryce the ostrich. What does he do again when he sees other birds flying? He cries. Imagine you are born as Bryce. You are so excited about your future because you think you'll be able to fly once you grow up. But day by day, you are starting to realize you are not meant to fly. You are not free as other birds. You live your whole life staying on the same ground and not being able to witness the beauty of the Earth from above.

How did you feel? Down? Frustrated? or Sympathetic? If what you felt was a feeling that is along the same lines, it means you have just projected a realistic emotion out of nothing but a thought. Because of that, you will now be able the remember Bryce every time you feel sad. The challenge in this application is combining the fanciful, exaggerated pictures with real, genuine emotions.

Now for a more comprehensive application, I need you to imagine the given scenario below and acquire all the feelings that will be mentioned. If you can pair each feeling with facial expression, then better.

Accelerated Learning

Scenario:

It's Monday morning and you woke up realizing you're late for work again; so, you hurriedly took a bath, slipped into your uniform, and rushed into the office. When you entered the office, you noticed that some people were staring at you—at your face, to be specific. Some started laughing and others started calling you Mona Lisa. You felt embarrassed. You went into the bathroom to see what was wrong. Apparently, you forgot to put on eyebrows. You began freaking out that you couldn't even leave the bathroom because you were ashamed of your sparse eyebrows.

While still being undecided inside the bathroom, you started hearing horses neighing from outside. You opened the door in shock as there were already thousands of armored soldiers, some riding horses, who are killing each other. "It's the Crusades!" Your officemate shouted. You saw one of the soldiers coming to you but you couldn't move your legs. He was about to slash you until "boom!" your boss had shot him before his sword could reach you. "Ha! I saved you with my gun!" your annoying boss braggingly claimed. "I invented this gunpowder, myself! You better thank me and my ingenious gunpowder invention," he added. Although you were more annoyed than grateful as he had always been that boastful, still, you thanked him. Then he left and joined the intensifying clash once again.

You hid under one of those tables in the office trying not get nearly slashed again. The whole building was filled with sounds of swords slashing. While you were hiding from those crusaders, you saw a mischief of car-sized rats coming from your boss' office. "Eww!" You shrieked in pure disgust. The rats began biting the crusaders and spread infectious disease inside the room. While the leader of the giant rats was busy shouting "bubonic plague!", you managed to find your way out of the building.

Shortly after leaving the office, you started seeing another horde of horsemen from afar approaching your location. One of your officemates, running from the same direction, was shouting "Run! It's the Mongol invasion!" You were frightened by what you have heard. But what scared you the most is when you realized the soldiers riding the horses were actually zombies. You started running again for your life but this time, faster.

You went straight to a newspaper publisher and reported everything. However, one of the employees there told you that your report could not be published until after three days because the printing press had just been invented that day. You got so disappointed after knowing that your report cannot be published on the same day. Hoping for another chance, you went to another newspaper publisher. The firm also rejected your report because the news that it was going to release for that day was about the spread of Islam. You started becoming angry because you felt like these publishers were intentionally ignoring your report. "Why can't you prioritize my news!?" you furiously shouted as you walk out of the establishment.

On your way home, you heard a sound of flapping wings from above. It seemed to you that those were just a couple of birds flying around until you looked up and saw a flying... money? A flying money! A lot of paper bills with wings were flying above you. You immediately thought that they might be your chance to become a millionaire. So, you excitedly chased after them. You were too focused on them that you bumped into a tree. "Oh no!" you shouted, realizing you lost track of the flying paper bills. You didn't know on which direction you could find them again. You looked around and then you saw an old man holding his compass. You stared at his compass in envy thinking that you would have been able to chase those bills if you only had one. Losing your hope, you decided to just return home and you slept the rest of the day.

Did the story make sense to you? I guess it didn't. But congrats, you have just had a run-through of the nine important events that happened during the post-classical era in our world history. If you tried feeling the action in the story genuinely, then you can easily remember each of the event stated through associating it with the specific feeling you had. To sum up the emotions and the corresponding information each of them represents:

- Embarrassment - the creation of Mona Lisa during Renaissance period

- Surprise - the crusades: the battle between Christianity and Islam

- Annoyance - gunpowder invention

- Disgust - the pandemic: bubonic plague

- Fear - Mongol Invasion

- Disappointment - invention of printing press

- Anger - spread of Islam

- Excitement - Tang dynasty introduces the flying money

- Envy - the invention of the navigational tool: compass

Chapter 8: Mind Mapping

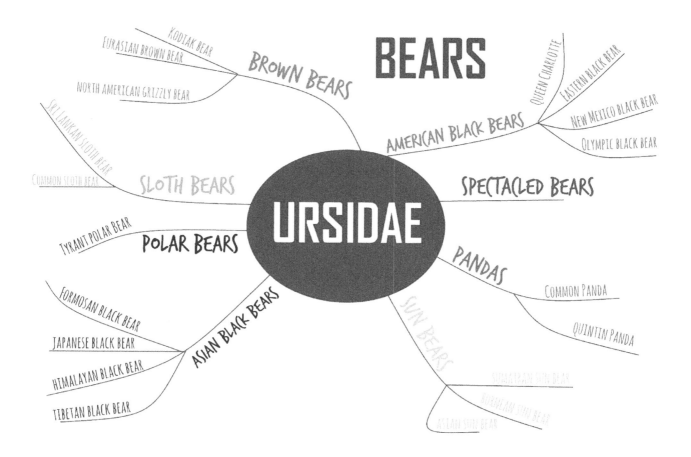

As you can see in the picture above, the details look like a bunch of stems sprouting from a seed in the center labeled as "Ursidae." Ursidae is the family name for bears. But since it is a too general term, another set of information, sprouting from the center, is created to specify the species under the family Ursidae. Majority of the eight species of this family however, still cover subspecies under them that is why the second level of information further sprouts to another level to specify each species' subspecies—and that is what we call a mind map.

Mind mapping is a method of memorization that uses a chart-like organization of information or simply, a mind map. It is typically used to highlight the relationships among the information being memorized. Thus, it organizes information in a better and more understandable way. Moreover, in mind mapping, the mind focuses on the image of the map, itself and not necessarily on the image of each of the information included in it. For this reason, no mental image is needed to represent each particular item in the map although it is not a hard and fast rule. There are some who prefer using images for each information so they can imagine a map containing images instead of words. In such case, the use of linking method is advised.

Creating a Mind Map

To create a mind map, you need to start with identifying which among the information you have is the center information. The center information, from the name itself, will serve as the center of the mind map. It is the subject that encompasses all the other ideas that will be included in the map. The center information is usually the topic or theme of the details you need to memorize or the title of the lesson in which the details are discussed. In the picture above, the center information is the family name of the bears.

After identifying the center, you need to come up with a second level of information directly connected to the center. Classify all the other information based on how close they are to the center information. That way, you will know the number of main topics you have and understand their relationship to the center information. They either have a common relationship to the center information—like what we have on the picture above—or are separately related to the center information. Regardless of which, they are still going to be included in the second level as long as they are the nearest connectible topic to the center. In the sample mind map we have, the second level information, sprouting directly from the center, is composed of the species under the bear family. They have a common relationship to the center because they are all subspecies. Now if we have other information like history of bears, famous bears in the world, and non-government organizations for the welfare of bears, the second level of information will not anymore enumerate the species on the second level and will only include the collective topic "species of bear" instead. And in that case, notice that the new main topics namely, history of bears, famous bears in the world, organizations for bears, and species of bears do not anymore have a common relationship toward the center information. Nonetheless, they all are still considered the nearest topics to the center information and shall therefore compose the second level.

Now that you have a center information and main topics, you need to choose which among the information left are being described or covered by each of the main topics. Note that the rest of the information you have are all probably related to the main topics but you need to filter the information with the nearest connection from the ones which can still be included under another level. In the picture above, the set of branches sprouting from every second level branch comprises the subspecies of each species of the bear family. The third level is generally composed of subtopics.

If you still have pieces of information left, you can just create and connect another set of branches from the existing branches to provided places for each information. Do this until all the information you need are covered. Just make sure that each information really does have a relationship with the branch from which it sprouts so you can visualize a smooth flow of connection among the items in the mind map.

You can visualize a mind map directly in your mind or you can draw it to a piece of paper first and subsequently familiarize yourself with the flow. Also, a mind map does not have to be presented the same way as the picture above. You can organize the information in a simpler and neater way although I must emphasize again that the weirder the image, the longer it stays in the mind. If the branches on your mind map look exactly the same, chances are the memories may overlap during retrieval and may lead to you, forgetting some of the information. But still, retention is at optimum level when you memorize in a way that you and your mind prefer.

Analyzing a Mind Map

Knowing now how information flows in a mind map, we can now properly translate the sample picture. There are eight species under the family Ursidae namely, the brown bears, sloth bears, polar bears, Asian black bears, sun bears, pandas, spectacled bears, and American black bears. The second level further sprouts into third-level branches which means the majority of these species still cover a set of subspecies. Thus, we can say that the Kodiak bear, Eurasian brown bear, and North American grizzly bear are the subspecies of the species brown bears. The subspecies of sloth bears, on the other hand, are Sri Lankan sloth bear and the common sloth bear. Polar bears had a subspecies named tyrant polar bear—although take note that it is already considered extinct today. The Asian black bears' subspecies include, though not limited to, Formosan black bear, Japanese black bear, Himalayan black bear, and Tibetan black bear. Sun bears have Asian sun bear, Bornean sun bear, and Sumatran sun bear as its subspecies. Subspecies under the species panda or giant panda are common panda and Quintin panda. Spectacled bears ended on the second level for they have no subspecies. Lastly, the subspecies of the American black bears include, but not limited to, Olympic black bear, New Mexico black bear, eastern black bear, and the Queen Charlotte black bear.

Organize Your Own Mind Map

Let's try another challenge but this time, you're going to create your own mind map. We're also not discussing about bears—we're going to meet the gods and goddesses of the famous Greek mythology. Although we are not going to cover the overwhelming number of all Greek mythology characters, the names may still confuse you. So, try to analyze relationships and visualize the connections as you read each detail. You may draw the mind map on a piece of paper and follow the flow of the relationships between these gods and goddesses or you may direct the visualization in your mind. The latter is more challenging and definitely more rewarding.

Starting with the first few greatest creations, Gaia, the personification of mother Earth, had a relationship with Uranus, the god of heavens. As a result of their love, twelve titans were born: Themis, the Titaness of divine law and order; Mnemosyne, the Titaness of memory; Hyperion, the titan of light; Theia, the Titaness of sight; Crius, the titan of constellations; Oceanus, the titan of the all-encircling river oceans; Tethys, the Titaness of fresh-water, Iapetus, the titan of mortality; Coeus, the titan of intellect; Phoebe, the Titaness of the prophecy; Cronus, the titan of harvests; and Rhea, the Titaness of fertility and motherhood. On the other hand, Aphrodite, the goddess of beauty and love was born through a sea foam from Uranus' genitals. It means she does not have any mother and the only parent she has is her father, Uranus.

Atlas, the titan who carried the heavens upon his shoulders was also born without a mother just like Aphrodite. He is the son of Iapetus. Oceanus and Tethys gave birth to Pleione, an Oceanid nymph. Coeus and Phoebe gave birth to Leto, the Titaness of motherhood. Cronus and Rhea, on the other hand, gave birth to the six renowned gods and goddesses: Zeus, the king of the gods, ruler of Mount Olympus, and the god of thunder; Hera, the queen of gods and the goddess of women; Poseidon, the god of the sea; Hestia, the virgin goddess of home; Hades, the god of the underworld and the dead; and Demeter, the goddess of harvest. Later on, Pleione and Atlas had an affair and resulted to the birth of Maia, the mother of Hermes.

Zeus, then began to produce his own children. He, and Semele gave birth to Dionysus. Zeus also had an affair with Maia who, as a result, gave birth to Hermes, the god of communication and trade. Zeus and Leto gave birth to the twin Olympians, Apollo and Artemis. Athena, the goddess of wisdom and battle strategy, also came from Zeus but without any mother. Lastly, Zeus and Hera gave birth to Ares, the god of war and violence, and Hephaestus, the god of metalworking and crafts.

You may now start drawing your own mind map. You may start by recalling the pieces of images you imagined while you were reading the story; and start organizing them based on relationships and sequence of existence. Form your own mind map and once you do, try to retell the story by yourself—then you'll know how helpful the mind map is.

Chapter 9: Visualizing Names

Getting to know a lot of people is all fun and games until you realize you cannot anymore remember all of their names. How can you? From your closest friends to the least noticed acquaintance, you are meant to know thousands of names in your life and it is impossible to remember all of them. You might be thinking that you are just not good at remembering people but actually, most of us feel the same thing too.

You might meet James Bond today or you might meet Nikolaj Coster-Waldau tomorrow. You really cannot know when a name is going to be easy and when it is going to be a burden. But cut the worries because one of the memorization techniques we have today are specifically developed to help people remember names. We'll call this technique as the connecting method since the bottom line of this method is to connect names with certain aspects. It is almost like the linking method except that we do not necessarily have a sequence of items to connect to each other but instead, we need to connect the information to itself. There are three bases to this method and any of which can be used to memorize names.

Appearance Connection

As you know, attention is significant in order to inject information in your mind. Your interest on someone instantly gives you the adequate amount of attention you need to be able to remember the name. If you try to pay the same level of attention to anybody, then you can possibly remember everyone's name. Appearance affects how much attention a person can provide that is why it is the first basis to the connecting method.

If you admire people because of their looks, chances are their names stick in your mind for a longer period. It is because you are fond of imagining their face at least once in a while that their names have been a part of your memory. If you ever had a crush on someone then you probably know what I'm talking about.

Come to think of it, even if you do not have personal interest or affection to some people, their names still stick in your memory because you can remember how these people appear. There are available mental images that correspond with the existence of the names in your mind; hence, you have both the names and the visuals. And that is actually the very point—you visualize.

If I introduce to you a person named Johnny Biggy, you'll probably forget about him just a few chapters after this exact moment. But if I describe him to you as a buff, blonde guy with curly hair who always wears a black leather coat and matches it with his funky metal earing on his right ear, you will be able to visualize him. Now the technique is, you do not need to force you brain to remember every description. Think about his surname "Biggy." Which among the descriptions I've given, may be linked or connected to such surname? The answer is his body figure. He's buff. You can label him in your mind as Johnny Biggy the buff. That way, you can remember him in an instant once you hear his name again.

Try to imagine a person named Jessica Bright as well. She's a woman of age 42 with a short hair who never forgets to apply sun screen to protect her white complexion. Now let's try to connect her name to the description. She's rich but it does not seem to have anything to do with her name. She's 42 but again, it has no impact to the mind. She has a white complexion. Now that's it. Her surname is Bright. Just imagine her shining so bright because of her white skin tone and most probably, you'll remember her for years.

Character Connection

Now what if Jessica Bright does not have a white complexion and she applies sun screen merely because she wants to protect her skin? You'll probably lose her name in an instant. However, if you find out that she's smart and holds a PhD in Mathematics, you will probably be able to remember her name again as Jessica is smart so she's bright; and therefore, she's Jessica Bright.

Accelerated Learning

The next option you have on which you can base your memory of people's names is their traits and characteristics. If appearance can affect attention, a person's character can affect emotions. Do you remember the person whom you hated before? Don't deny it. We all have hated people before, most especially when we were still young and couldn't comprehend everything that other people did. Your hate, or basically any other feeling toward people is most probably influenced by their character. You admire smart people, get angry with bad people, and get happy when you are with funny people. You can easily remember the names of the people whose characters have had an impact to your life at least once.

The good news is that you don't have to meet and be with people every day just so you can remember their names. You just need to connect the traits they have with their names in any way possible. For example, the name Shawn Fury may not sound something your mind can remember for weeks. But if we connect it to one of his characteristics, then your mind might consider letting the name rest in your memory for a while. So, let's discuss about Shawn Fury. Shawn Fury is a head of a certain office's department. He is also smart like Jessica Bright although he's a slowpoke. He loves watching movies, playing chess, and yelling at his subordinates every time they do not meet his expectation. Also, he's rich and he fosters seventeen stray cats in his house. To connect, his first name Shawn does not really have a connection with any part of the description. But, his last name Fury has one—the fact that he loves yelling at his subordinates when they do not work the way he expects them to be. He is always angry so you can say he is Shawn "Furious" and your mind shall remember the name Shawn Fury.

Two-word names are actually easy to remember but unfortunately, that is not the common case. What if you meet someone whose name is Agatha Sherry Marie Routundder Smith? Don't panic. You should try to get to know her first. Agatha, despite his femininity, has a loud, deep voice. She loves performing on stage. In fact, she is a great dancer and theater actress. She always eats during class although she's clearly not that generous as she does not share her food no matter what. She also does not study much, perhaps because she is an active officer of one of their school's organization. With her active campus life, she often forgets about taking care of herself. She usually enters the room with a stained dress, or attends in class with her hair uncombed.

Among the given characteristics, which do you think will help you remember her name? If you do not have any answer nor a clue, then analyze how some of her characters are connected to her name. Agatha has a loud, deep voice and that can be represented by the sound of a thunderclap which is loud and deep as well. Notice that the fourth word in her name is Routundder. We can link the term "raw thunder" to it and make it sound like the actual pronunciation of the name Routundder. So, Agatha has a loud and deep voice that sounds like a raw thunder which also sounds like Routundder. Another characteristic that we can connect to Agatha is her messy habit of not grooming herself. She looks like she's working in a factory, or in a smithy. Yep, smithy as in her surname Smith. So, you can remember her by visualizing a girl named Agatha Sherry Marie with a voice of a Raw Thunder who works in a Smithy.

Meeting Place Connection

The meeting place is the most realistic basis among the three bases for connecting names to people. Actual settings like park, school, supermarket, club, beach, and any other place can potentially trigger a memory that may depict either a scene or an image of a certain person. Meeting place connection does not require you to visualize a projected image because the place through which you can remember the person already exists. This technique is done by simply remembering the place where you met the specific person and associating it with the same person's name.

You've met Johnny Biggy, Jessica Bright, Shawn Fury, and Agatha Sherry Marie Routundder Smith in this book so you can say they are somehow counted. However, you may test your memory in a better way through a more realistic approach. You may speak of a certain place and observe if your mind can produce a name or names. The names that your mind will produce are most probably the names of the people whom you met or usually see in the stated place.

The bases you've learned are not strictly independent to each other. This means you can use a combination of any two or all to remember a person's name if that is what fits the situation the most. However, always bear in your mind that as much as possible, you need to single out the most practical basis among the three. If you can clearly remember a person's name through visualizing the place where you met that person, then do not struggle for connecting his name to another basis. No matter how large your memory is, if you do not know how to efficiently store information then its capacity will always seem so limited to you.

Chapter 10: Visualizing Numbers (Major System)

Most people find numbers as the hardest to memorize. Unlike letters, numbers cannot form words when combined nor form a mental image when read. Memorizing two to three digits is considerable while four to six digits are fine; but having to memorize seven to fifteen digits is punishing unless the digits are your own phone number. They can even form a 370-digit number and still be considered as a valid value. The thing is, numbers are infinite and that's what makes it confusing.

Major System

The pegs under the number rhyme and number shape systems replace the numbering on a certain list; thus, they, themselves represent numbers. For this reason, these systems are not your best choice for memorizing numbers since they may only lead to confusion. In such case, you may opt to use the major system. It is a peg system which replaces single-digit numeric values with sounds of letters or phonemes. Through it, any combination of numbers forming more than one digits will also be able to form different words and sounds.

0 = /s/ /z/ and /x/

1 = /t/ /d/ /θ/ and /ð/

2 = /n/

3 = /m/

4 = /r/

5 = /l/

6 = /ʃ/ /tʃ/ /dʒ/ /ʒ/

7 = /c/ /k/ hard g /q/

8 = /f/ /v/

9 = /p/ /b/

From the summarized list above, notice that each digit is represented by letters and symbols. So how is each letter or symbol connected to its corresponding digit? Let's start with zero (0). The easiest way to remember the letters for zero is through its first letter. Zero begins with the sound of *z* as in "zealous". Therefore, it also covers the sounds near to it like the sounds of *s* as in "snake" and *x* as in "xylophone".

The sounds associated with number one (1), on the other hand, is represented by letters written with a single vertical stroke each. Letters *t* and *d*, therefore, are the same with *1* which also only has one vertical stroke. The sounds of *t* as in "technique" and *d* as in "dog" are also relatively close to the sounds of *th* (θ) as in "thorn" and *th* (ð) as in "those." So, *th* (θ) and *th* (ð) are still included in the sounds and letters linked to number one.

The letters for numbers two to five are easier to remember. Two (2) is represented by *n* as in "night" because the letter *n* is written with two vertical strokes. Three (3), on the other hand, is represented by *m* as in "mammoth" as *m* contains three vertical strokes. Four (4) takes *r* as its symbol simply because it ends with the sound of *r* as in "rabbit." Five (5) is associated with *l* as in "Lamborghini" because in the system of Roman numeral, the number 50 is represented by L.

The number six (6) almost looks like the letter *G*, as well as the lower-case *g* when flipped both vertically and horizontally. Thus, six is the digit for the all the soft *g* sounds like gym and gesture. The sounds that are also covered by the number six are *j* (dʒ) as in "jump," *sh* (ʃ) as in "sure," *ch* (tʃ) as in "chimney," and the sound of *z* (ʒ) in "seizure."

The hard *g* sound like "goat" falls under the number seven (7). It also includes the sounds of *c* as in "caramel," *k* as in "karate," *q* as in "queue," and the sound of *ch* in "loch." Eight (8), on the other hand, covers the sounds of *f* and *ph* as in "free" and "phone." Sounds like *v* in "love" and *gh* in "laugh" also fall under the number eight.

To remember the letters and sounds for nine (9), just think of the letter *P* flipped horizontally or a lower-case *b* rotated 180°. The sounds of these letters, *p* as in "page" and *b* as in "baboon," are what represent the number nine. The vowels *a e i o u* and other consonants like *h y* and *w* are not assigned to any digit; hence, no value. They can be used to fill consonants to form a word without changing its value.

Usage

Using the summarized list, we can form any word that will make us remember the number to which it is linked. If I give you the word "hair" then you can tell it is a word for 4. The consonant *h* and the vowels *a* and *i* do not have any value but the letter *r* has. So, spelling out the letters in the word "hair" through their designated values, it is going to appear as 0004 or simply, 4. The word "owl" can be translated into 005 or 5 while the word "ham" is equal to 003 or 3.

Do not confuse the undesignated letters and sounds with those that represent the number zero. The word "may" is equivalent to 3-0-0, or when simplified becomes 3 while the word "max" may also be written as 3-0-0 but, when simplified, becomes 30. The two zeros in the word "may" come from the vowel *a* and consonant *y* which means they are not actual zeros and do not have any value under this system. However, only one of the two zeros in the word "max" has no value and it comes from the vowel *a*. *X*, on the other hand, is equal to an actual zero.

Accelerated Learning

A word may also be formed containing two or more digits like "cheek" which is composed of ch-e-e-k or 6-0-0-7 or 67. "Metal" may be translated as 315. You can also form your own words by yourself using several combinations. For example, given the values 7 and 9 we can form words like cape or cope (7090) and pace (9070). Of course, if a value is composed of numbers in strict order, the choices will be limited. If we have 900941, the only single word we can form is "passport."

It is important to remember that unlike the other peg systems, the major system restricts the system to the given corresponding letters and sounds for each digit. So, you cannot change it based on what you prefer more. However, the words you can form through each digit or combination of digits are certainly up to you.

Sample words from 1-50:

1   tea (1-0-0 = 1)

2   hen (0-0-2 = 2)

3   ham (0-0-3 = 3)

4   ray (4-0-0 = 4)

5   wheel (0-0-0-0-5 = 5)

6   show (6-0-0 = 6)

7   hike (0-0-7-0 = 7)

8   wife (0-0-8-0 = 8)

9   wipe (0-0-9-0 = 9)

10   dose (1-0-0-0 = 10; again, do not confuse actual zeros with zeros that do not have value)

11   toad (1-0-0-1 = 11)

12 tune (1-0-2-0 = 12)

13 doom (1-0-0-3 = 13)

14 deer (1-0-0-4 = 14)

15 tool (1-0-0-5 = 15)

16 teach (1-0-0-6 = 16)

17 twice (1-0-0-7-0 = 17)

18 dive (1-0-8-0 = 18)

19 dub (1-0-9 = 19)

20 Nazi (2-0-0-0 = 20)

21 note (2-0-1-0 = 21)

22 neon (2-0-0-2 = 22)

23 enemy (0-2-0-3-0 = 23)

24 honor (0-0-2-0-4 = 24)

25 inhale (0-2-0-0-5-0 = 25)

26 nacho (2-0-6-0 = 26)

27 niece (2-0-0-7-0 = 27)

28 naive (2-0-0-8-0 = 28)

29 nap (2-0-9 = 29)

30 max (3-0-0 = 30)

31 meadow (3-0-0-1-0-0 = 31)

32 moon (3-0-0-2 = 32)

33 mime (3-0-3-0 = 33)

34 more (3-0-4-0 = 34)

35 mole (3-0-5-0 = 35)

36   mash (3-0-6 = 36)

37   mug (3-0-7 = 37)

38   movie (3-0-8-0-0 = 38)

39   mop (3-0-9 = 39)

40   erase (0-4-0-0-0 = 40)

41   road (4-0-0-1 = 41)

42   urine (4-0-0-2 = 42)

43   rum (4-0-3 = 43)

44   aurora (0-0-4-0-4-0 = 44)

45   royal (4-0-0-0-5 = 45)

46   rush (4-0-6 = 46)

47   rake (4-0-7-0 = 47)

48   wharf (0-0-0-4-8 = 48)

49   herb (0-0-4-9 = 49)

50   lazy (5-0-0-0 = 50)

Common Mistakes

Bear in mind that major system can lead to wrongful translations when not correctly used. The most common problem people commit when using this system is the addition of an extra sound to the word that is supposed to represent an exact combination of digits. So, you don't represent the number 17 with the word "duct" as it has an extra t sound at the end and therefore represents the number 171 (1+0+7+1).

Another common mistake is doubling the letter inside a word when not necessary. You cannot simply replace the word "diner" with "dinner" just because they both have the sound n in the middle. It can cause confusion as diner represents 124 (1+0+2+0+4) while dinner translates into 1224 (1+0+2+2+0+4). Refrain from doing such practice as it may lead to confusion most especially during exams.

Lastly, the most important thing to remember in major system is that it is about the sounds and not necessarily the letters. The word "place," when decoded shall result to 950 (9+5+n+0+n). The letter c takes the sound of s under the digit 0 and not the c under the digit 7. Thus, it should not be translated as 957 (9+5+n+7+n)

Notice that among all the memorization techniques, this system implements the strictest rules and specifications. But it is only because it prevents the confusion among the representations as confusion is exactly the problem why numbers are hard to memorize. Still, the major system is the greatest tool you can use when it comes to dealing with numbers.

Chapter 11: Visualizing Numbers (Other Systems)

The major system is generally the best choice when it comes to memorizing any given set of numbers. However, if you cannot find your way yet to master the major system technique, you may choose to settle first with other less extensive, but almost as effective, techniques of dealing with numbers. Although it is the major system that can dramatically improve your flexibility in memorizing numbers, it will be best for you if you first try the simpler methods and then just work your way to mastering the major system. Methods like chunking and the PAO system adopt less strict rules to simplify the process of memorization.

Chunking System

The easiest way to remember a set of various digits is through chunking. It is basically dividing a long number into chunks of either two, three, or four digits, to remember the set as a collection of groups of numbers and not as a single group of many digits. You may have noticed before that your phone number, PIN number, and other important numbers are presented with divisions or groupings. It is actually an example of chunking. It doesn't just divide numbers. It makes the numbers look more organized and therefore easier to remember.

For example, you need to memorize the number 343189563231. Just by looking at it, your eyes might already be hurting. To avoid the feeling of getting overwhelmed by a 12-digit number, let's try chunking it into six groups:

34-31-89-56-32-31

Through chunking, you can now read it as thirty-four, thirty-one, eighty-nine, fifty-six, thirty-two, and thirty-one. Thus, chunking also makes the number easier to read and pronounce.

However, grouping the digits by twos may not be practical most especially when you are given a longer set. Therefore, let's try to chunk it into four groups:

343-189-563-231

You may memorize it now as three hundred forty-three, one hundred eighty-nine, five hundred sixty-three, and two hundred thirty-one. Observe that the terms from translating number into words may have lengthen a bit but they are actually fewer this time. If under the six-group chunks you read six separate numbers, in here you read only four separate numbers. If you want to make it less, you can divide the set into three chunks:

3431-8956-3231

So, it is now read as three thousand four hundred thirty-one, eight thousand nine hundred fifty-six, three thousand two hundred thirty-one. The number of digits in a chunk typically ranges from one to four. Five or more chunks may already lose the sense of chunking since they still seem a bulk of unmemorizable number. Also remember that as much as possible, start the division from the last digits so the first chunk will contain the least number of digits in case there is uneven distribution. To demonstrate, you are given the 11-digit password 20685485471. You cannot evenly distribute the numbers into chunks of two, three, nor four. So, if you decide to use the four-digit chunks, it shall be rewritten as 206-8548-5471.

Decoding Chunks using Major System

To practice the application of the major system on the chunking method, let's try to decipher a long set of numbers. At this point, we can now apply both the chunking method and the major system to decipher numbers that are composed of a lot of digits. You may divide the digits into a certain number of chunks depending on your preference. Let's use this 20-digit passcode as an example:

13219540947001886751

Distributing the set into two-digit chunks, you'll get:

13-21-95-40-94-70-01-88-67-51

After chunking, assign a word to each chunk using the representational codes under the major system. Make sure that what you assign to a single chunk is also a single word as much as possible as assigning more than two words to a single chunk does not sound practical. Besides, you are chunking to make memorization easier and not to memorize longer sentences. To help you form and assign words, presented below is the major system's summary of codes:

0 = /s/ /z/ and /x/

1 = /t/ /d/ /θ/ and /ð/

2 = /n/

3 = /m/

4 = /r/

5 = /l/

6 = /ʃ/ /tʃ/ /dʒ/ /ʒ/

7 = /c/ /k/ hard g /q/

8 = /f/ /v/

9 = /p/ /b/

Now let's try to make words out of the chunks we have:

13 - team

21 - neat

95 - blue

40 - horse

94 - pair

70 - case

01 - haste

88 - off

67 - jog

51 - late

You may just memorize the sequence of words assigned to the chunks although if you want to make things easier, you may visualize a scenario covering all the words assigned in sequence. Let's say, your team is not color blue and the horse is not your pair. In your case, you must haste to jump off and jog because you're late. The scene created honestly sounds weird but your mind can easily remember it; hence, it makes the number easy to remember.

Notice, however, that the sentence is quite long to memorize. So, let's try to chunk the set again but this time, we chunk it by threes:

13-219-540-947-001-886-751

Assigning words to each chunk we have: doom is when your honeydew lawyers brook the sixth huffish cloud. Remember, your first word represents only two-digit numbers since the first chunk always gets the least number of digits in case the set is not distributable evenly; so, get used to it. If you feel like you can get a simple and easier sentence, then you may distribute the set into four-digit chunks:

1321-9540-9470-0188-6751

Dominate the players because they practice all stuff with chocolate. A sentence that is as simple as that can already make you remember a 20-digit passcode. Therefore, chunks of three digits or four digits are more convenient and efficient to use.

PAO System

The combination of chunking and major systems actually explains how the PAO system works. PAO is an acronym that stands for Person-Action-Object system. It's a systematic way of forming a sentence that is literally composed of a person, an action, and an object. Through this technique, visualization of a single scenario that exhibits exactly what the sentence explains, can already make you remember a combination of six digits.

Like the major system, PAO system works best if you create your preliminary list of pegs although PAO is composed of not only one, but three sets of lists. You should also understand that PAO uses the same set of representational codes coming from other systems—in this case, from the major system. To demonstrate, consider the sample list of pegs below:

Number	Person	Action	Object
21	Nath	note	nut
40	Rose	hears	horse
58	Lovey	leave	loaf

From the list above, we can say that Nath note the nut is a sentence for number 21. Notice that it doesn't have to follow the strict grammar rules as it may alter the words and result to confusion. 40, on the other hand, may be translate into Rose hears the horse and 58 may be remembered as Lovey leave the loaf.

If you need to chunk a long number, make sure that each chunk consists the same number of digits as what you have on your list. Since the pegs above represent two-digit numbers, you need to divide a long number into chunks of two digits. If you have 405821, then you should divide it as 40-58-21. Now how is PAO system applied here?

The first chunk takes the person peg; so, the number 40 takes the name Rose. The second chunk takes the action; thus, 58 takes the action hears. The third chunk then takes the object; so, 21 takes the object nut. To translate 405821, we can use the sentence, "Rose hears the nut."

If your number is composed of more than six digits, you need to divide the number first into groups of six before diving each group into chunks of two. That means if you have 309845317234, you have to rewrite it as 30-98-45 and 31-72-34. In such case, you need to memorize two sentences to memorize the digits.

Chapter 12: Memory Palace

For centuries, mnemonists claim the palace method as the greatest memorization technique. It is also called the loci or the journey method as it somehow allows the user to "journey" through his memory storage. Renowned for its dramatic effects on the memory, people up until this age utilize the use of this technique to memorize almost anything. But how does the palace method exactly work?

The palace method uses a virtual storage called the memory palace. The memory palace is any place or structure that serves as a storage of information. It only exists in the mind and can take any form of structure such as a house, an office, a market, or anything. It can be as small as a closet or as huge as an actual palace. It can be as simple as a room or as complex as a maze. It can also take the form of an existing place. As a matter of fact, a lot of mnemonists use their own houses as their memory palace.

The purpose of the memory palace is to provide a space through which a person can travel and retrieve his memory. Yes, you can virtually travel through the memory palace and consciously retrieve memories from it. It's like a locker where you can safekeep your things and get them whenever they are needed, except that it's a large, walk-in locker. You can place any information in the form of a mental image at a specific place or position inside the memory palace. Visualizing and connecting the mental image to its place or position will ease the retrieval of the information.

Scenario:

I'm going to describe a place and I need you to visualize every detail clearly as we are going to enter a room. On the doorstep is a brown, dusty doormat that says "please leave your shoes there," with an arrow pointing on the left, where the shoe rack is located. The entrance is not that wide but is enough to allow two people to enter. Three steps from the door, on the left is a small bathroom. Walking further, there is a red, medium-sized sofa facing the television set. Immediately at the right of the sofa is a wooden study desk with three drawers below and a small lampshade on it. Between the sofa and the tv is a glass table on a golden-brown carpet. Next to the tv set, on its left, stands an old, dirty white refrigerator and just beside it is the sink. That's it. You've just had a tour around a memory palace.

Designing Your Own Memory Palace

Structure   Memory palace is not just an empty room where you can dump information and retrieve them. It has to have details. It has to both look and feel real. Now you might be thinking that creating a memory palace is just an additional burden to memorize. Well, actually, the thing you need to remember in constructing your memory palace is familiarity.

The reason a lot of mnemonists use their own house is because they are already familiar with it. There's no memorization needed. You just have to visualize your own house. If you don't want to use your house, then make sure that the place you are going to use as a memory palace should be, as much as possible, a place you are very familiar to.

Size   The size of the palace also matters. It has to be spacious enough so you can feel like you are indeed, travelling. It should not be too narrow but it shouldn't also be too wide. If the place is too narrow, it means you cannot walk around it. If it's too wide, then that means the place seems empty and you are not maximizing the space available. Just make sure you can "walk around" the place and that shall be enough.

Complexity The complexity, on the other hand, plays an important role in the capacity of the memory palace. Details, in the form of furniture, appliances, or designs in the house should be realistic as they are the specific places or positions in which you can put information. The directions, on the other hand, should not in any case add to your confusion. The sections, divisions, and directions within the structure should allow you to navigate the place freely. It doesn't matter if the memory palace is as complex as a maze. As long as you are familiar to it and you can travel around without getting lost, that's completely fine.

The reason you have to regard the familiarity of structure, spaciousness of size, and the level of complexity when it comes to building a memory palace is that they make "navigating" the mind easy. Notice that we are using words like walk, travel, and navigate as if we are talking about an actual place; but as far as the palace method is concerned, these words simply mean to think of or to recall a memory. To further understand how memory palace works, let's try to encode the list below:

Party Foods:

- pizza
- red wine
- buffalo wings
- burger
- popcorn
- chicken nuggets
- cake
- brownies
- ribs
- fries
- lasagna

- bacon strips

- cookies

- soda

Since, most probably you haven't designed your own memory palace yet, let's just use the room that was previously described. Entering the room, the first detail we can use as a specific storage for a single information is the brown, dusty doormat. To connect both the place and information, you can imagine the doormat is a one, rectangular slice of pizza. The next detail available shall be the shoe rack so imagine the shoe rack containing red wines tied with shoe laces instead of ribbons. Walking in, imagine you hear a buffalo singing inside the bathroom as you pass by it. That shall connect the buffalo wings to the bathroom.

Now, imagine the sofa as a huge burger and the show on tv is about producing popcorn. Also picture a chicken sitting on the study desk (chicken nuggets) staring at the cake beside it. Imagine the cake having a birthday lampshade on it instead of a candle. Since the desk has three drawers, we can use these drawers to place a total of three information. Imagine the pull or knob of the top drawer is colored brown (brownies). The second one's knob, on the other hand, is a bone (ribs) while that of the third drawer is made of potato (fries).

Replace the glass table with a huge lasagna and the carpet with large bacon strips. After then, imagine the ref's door bombarded with cookie magnets. Lastly, imagine the faucet on the sink producing soda instead of water.

After you placing each information in its place, try to imagine reentering the room and see if you can retrieve all the items. If you can, then that means you did the palace method correctly. If you cannot recall all the scenarios, just keep on practicing. Remember, the palace method does not rely heavily on the retrieval process; as it is all about the encoding of information.

Make sure that you place information in specified details and that you visualize each connection properly.

Random Pick Up

To prove the flexibility of this method, try to answer the following questions based on the set of information we've just placed:

- The singing you hear from the bathroom every time you walk past it represents what food?
- What does the faucet on the sink produce?
- The lampshade is on what food?
- The table was replaced by what food?
- What does the show on tv represent?

If you have answered all the questions just by reimagining the memory palace, then you have just proven the method's flexibility. Using the memory palace, you can retrieve information properly even without recalling the sequence. Like when you were asked what the faucet produces, you can certainly proceed to where the sink is placed, and immediately connect the faucet with soda. In other words, you can remember the soda without first reciting all the other things on the list that come before it.

Memory palace does not just help you visualize information. Is also helps expand your retention capacity. You also get to enjoy the feeling of being able to "travel" inside your memory. Keep on practicing this method and for sure, you will master memorization eventually.

Conclusion

From all the tricks and techniques you have learned, we can now redefine photographic memory as the ability to consistently use visualization to form memory visuals through the use of various techniques and methods.

That definitely sounds more realistic and achievable. However, you should remember that regardless of how you define it, the most important thing is that you have learned the techniques to improve your memory. After all, these techniques are your true achievement.

You are now aware of the link or linking system which is best for memorizing details in order. You are now also knowledgeable with the peg systems covering the number rhyme, number shape, and the alphabet peg systems; as well as the major and PAO systems that are specially developed to memorize numbers. Also, you now know about the emotion-based system wherein you can also practice connecting your feelings to your visuals.

If you love organizing information before memorizing them, then you may now opt to use the mind map method. To remember names, you can now apply the connecting method. And above all, to memorize any kind and any set of information, you now know where to go—the memory palace.

All these techniques that you have learned, when frequently used, will not only improve your speed in memorizing information but will also expand your memory. Having a great memory is not a matter of birth, but a matter of hard work. So, keep on practicing! And in case you're wondering where to start, remember that long number you skipped in the introduction? Try decoding it using the major system.

Book - III

Mindfulness

7 Secrets to Stop Worrying, Eliminate Stress, and Finding Peace with Mindfulness and Meditation

Introduction

I want to thank you and congratulate you for downloading the book, "Mindfulness: 7 Secrets to Stop Worrying, Eliminate Stress and Finding Peace with Mindfulness and Meditation".

This book contains proven steps and strategies on how to receive the benefits of the practice of mindfulness so you can live in ubiquitous peace.

We all have found ourselves stuck in the middle of the whirlwind of our thoughts and uncontrolled emotions. The only difference is that some know how to step into the clear, while some will find themselves transported to far places. Let this book be your guide that will show you how to never get tangled between your feelings and thoughts ever again.

From what it is and why bother practicing it, to revealing you the secrets that will jumpstart this relaxing journey of yours, this book will transform your life and bring order to your overburdened mind.

There are many great books on mindfulness, so why should you buy this one? The answer is simple – because this is not a book that will try to convince you to become mindful. This is a book that allows you to experience the rewards that the mindfulness provide, first hand.

Thanks again for purchasing this book, I hope you enjoy it!

Chapter 1: The 'Here' And 'Now'

Don't you just hate it when you watch a good movie and you have to fast backward because you have suddenly realized you have no idea what is going on? Does that ever happen to you? To be flooded by a rain of thoughts when all you want to do is sit and relax? If only there was a way to clean our minds from the unimportant stuff that only clutters our brain. And while it is impossible to give our brains a bath, there is a way for us to pay attention to the present, fully focused. No, I am not talking about taking some stimulant that will cause brain damage. I am talking about something that comes from within. I am talking about *mindfulness.*

Living mindfully, mindfulness meditation... Go to a bookstore and skim through a few books on alternative medicine, energy healing or even concentration boosting, chances are the word 'mindfulness' will pop up sooner rather than later. Health experts and spirituality gurus are talking about this term constantly. I, personally, don't know a single person who hasn't heard of mindfulness. But do they all really know what exactly is mindfulness? If they really did, I am sure they would all have been living in peace and serenity. Because that is what mindfulness is all about. Reaching deep and finding your inner peace.

Although its roots are set in the ancient Buddhism, the Western world got properly introduced to mindfulness, when in 1979, professor Jon Kabat Zinn took the spiritual part out of this practice and presented the American mainstream the secular mindfulness technique. After years of carefully studying the mindfulness practice, he shaped it into something that people in the West could also relate to. A practice that Americans didn't see as something 'exotic'. Today, there are millions of people from all over the world who have improved their lives thanks to his devotion. He gave us the possibility to learn how to live *here and now.*

The mindfulness practice offers a way for us to disengage from the overthinking, the worries and emotional burdens in our life. At the heart of the mindfulness, there is the art of paying attention. According to Jon Kabat Zan, paying attention to the things that surround you is the only way you can truly learn how to be happy. But how do we pay attention? Is acknowledging the rainy day enough? Here is what most people get wrong. They confuse awareness with mindfulness. I have found that these two different concepts are often interchanged, which is really incorrect. Being simply aware of something and being mindful about it, are two very different states of mind. Let me explain this a little bit better. Let's say that you are a grumpy person. After some time, and probably after being called that way frequently, you become aware that you are in fact grumpy. That is awareness. But awareness stops right there. Think of it as a step in the process of becoming mindful. You merely acknowledge the truth and it all ends there. You don't try to work on your character. You do not bother to find out what triggers you to act that way, let alone try to overcome it. But, that can be done through mindfulness. Mindfulness can help you change the way you act, by freeing your overloaded mind, letting go of the worries and enjoying simply being.

Mindfulness is defined as the state of paying attention in these three different ways:

Paying attention ON PURPOSE. Doing things purposefully is the first and the most important part of the practice of mindfulness. Our conscious plays a major role in our way to becoming mindful since our deliberate actions are more than required for us to become aware of what is going on around us. On purpose, means to consciously place our attention where we want. If we want to finish our work project on time, we purposefully place our attention solely on the task we have to complete.

Paying attention IN THE PRESENT. If left on its own, our mind will start wandering to the most distant places. Besides that, it is obviously nothing more, but unproductive and a real time-waster, not being in the present adds up to our inner tension and causes us more stress. Now, imagine being able to stay in the present without wasting your time worrying about the things you should have done differently. Being mindful means not dwelling on the past nor preparing for the future, but really, experiencing the present.

Paying attention NON JUDGMENTALLY. Although this is probably the trickiest part of all, being able to observe the things without judging them can indeed be achieved, even if it seems impossible at this stage. When practicing mindfulness, we are not trying to gain control over our thoughts, but simply observe them non judgmentally. The most important part of observing without judging, is not to get caught up with thoughts or emotions, but simply understand that they are there. With this practice, we can learn how to mechanically dispute the negativity and open up to freedom.

You cannot possibly hope to become mindful if you have no idea what mindfulness is all about. Now that you have learned what the cornerstone of this practice is, let me reveal to you the secret of how you can truly benefit from it.

Chapter 2: Reap the Benefits

Imagine your junk drawer. Now, be honest and admit that you have one. Everyone does. You know, that one drawer where you hide all of your junk when you have guests coming over. The drawer where you can find anything from your lighter and metro card, to the I-have-been-looking-for-this-since-forever kind of items. Imagine you are trying to find something you have stored there last week. So, somewhere between the emptying and bringing items back to the drawer, you realize that it would have been a lot easier if the drawer was organized. The same example can be used to explain the mindfulness. Without it, your mind is no different than your junk drawer. Cluttered and overloaded with unimportant things. This practice helps you bring order to it. Mindfulness can help you achieve your goals without having to push aside the 'junk' thoughts. Practicing mindfulness is highly beneficial.

Since the world has been introduced to the practice of mindfulness, thousands of researches and studies have been performed, all with one goal – to see how mindfulness affects our health, both mentally and physically. All of them can agree that even after only a couple of weeks of successfully practicing this technique, a person can experience some amazing psychological, physical and social benefits and have a significantly increased life satisfaction. Isn't that the sole purpose of living?

The pace in which we live our lives calls for some serious changes. The amount of stress we encounter on a daily basis can really take a toll on our overall health. Fortunately, simply implementing mindfulness in our life can drag a bunch of improvements and enhance it. And the best part? The benefits that we can experience while practicing it have been backed by science.

Besides the obvious benefits such as improving the focus, gaining awareness, decreasing stress, relieving anxiety and boosting the concentration, the practice of mindfulness can improve your life on so many different levels:

Mindfulness can improve the mood.

Did you know that mindfulness is considered to be a very important factor in achieving happiness? Through this practice, one gains a meaningful appreciation even for the small things in life, which leads to improving the well-being. Studies have proven that practicing mindfulness can help a person stay alert even in some very stressful situations like going off to war. One research performed on soldiers who were preparing for deployment, have shown that those who practiced mindfulness had a much more positive mood, unlike those who weren't mindful and were way too emotional and scared.

Mindfulness can ease the pain.

Have you heard the expression 'it's all in your head'? While it is mostly used when we want to tell a person that he is imagining things, this old saying is sometimes used when a person is in pain. Although it may not be entirely true, a study has shown that a significant part of the pain we experience in the back, neck, and some other body parts may only be in our heads. The same study, published in the Journal of Neuroscience has found that mindfulness meditation can ease the aches and cut our pain by an amazing 50%.

Mindfulness can increase the immune function.

Since it was introduced to the Western culture, many hospitals started to encourage their patients to practice mindfulness. Among the multiple benefits that the mindfulness can reward us with, is the fact that it can boost our immune system and here is how. The antibodies that are produced by our immune system are in charge for destroying viruses. When we are stressed, we allow the stress to decrease the production of the antibodies, making us more vulnerable to viruses. Mindfulness relieves us from the stress and therefore, contributes to improving the immune function. A certain study has shown that after an 8-week mindfulness training, the participants showed an incredible increase in the antibodies, and enhanced their function.

Mindfulness can slow down neurodegenerative conditions.

The progression of dementia, Alzheimer's and other age-related cognitive diseases can be significantly slowed down if the person who is affected by such a disorder practices mindfulness, a study performed at the Beth Israel Deaconess Medical Center has shown. After 8 weeks of practicing this beneficial technique, the participants showed some amazing improvements.

Mindfulness can reduce addiction.

Having such a great impact on the self-control areas in the brain, it is no surprise that mindfulness can also reduce addiction and help people give up their bad habits such as drinking or smoking. A study performed on smokers who were practicing mindfulness meditation and another group of smokers who were following a program formed by the American Lung Association that was supposed to help them to stop smoking, has shown that those who practiced mindfulness were much more likely to quit smoking, than the other group.

Mindfulness can prevent cellular aging.

We have all heard at least one story of a Chinese monk who used to live for hundreds of years. Although these kinds of tales are usually exaggerated, here is a fact that we all (women especially) will find useful – mindfulness meditation can slow down the aging process. You better throw away the no-wrinkles creams and purchase a meditation cushion, since many studies have proven that mindfulness meditation slows down the progression of our cells' aging.

Mindfulness can lower the high blood pressure.

A research published in the Journal of Bio Behavioral Medicine has found out that people suffering from borderline high blood pressure can significantly reduce it, if they practice mindfulness. The participants followed a mindfulness stress reduction training program and showed some incredible improvements at the end.

Mindfulness can boost creativity.

A study performed by the researchers at the Leiden University found that the practice of mindfulness can significantly improve the divergent and cognitive thinking that are the most important factors of creativity. The participants who were aware and in the enhanced their creativity considerably.

Mindfulness can strengthen relationships.

Although there is no way that the mindfulness, or any other practice for that matter, to have a direct effect on the relationships in your life, many other benefits you will most likely receive through mindfulness such as increased empathy, compassion and loving attitude, will definitely reward you with strong relationships.

Mindfulness can make us feel less lonely.

A study performed on 40 older participants has found that if we practice mindfulness meditation for 30 minutes every day for 8 weeks, we will reduce our feelings of loneliness.

The practice of mindfulness can also:

Decrease inflammatory disorders

Help us live longer

Increase our tolerance levels

Increase resilience

Help us make decisions

Make us smarter

Improve our sex life

Improve our sleep

Decrease the risk of depression

Decrease the risk of cardiovascular diseases

Support our goal to lose weight

Improve the skin resistance

Prevent asthma and so much more

The most amazing part about these benefits that one can acquire through the practice of mindfulness, is the fact that a person does not have to be actively practicing it in order to be able to reap the advantages that the mindfulness offer. It is truly incredible how through the act of practicing mindfulness, long-term changes in our brain are made, so even when not sitting in a lotus position or practicing walking mindfulness meditation, the practitioner will still be rewarded with these multiple benefits.

Chapter 3: From Auto to Manual

"It is only when you wake up that you realize you were sleeping" – unknown.

From the moment we wake up until we hug our pillows at night, our day is filled with all kinds of different tasks. And on most days, these tasks are almost identical. Think about it, brushing teeth, showering, eating, and even working – we are used to doing these things, and most of the time, we don't give them that much of attention. That is all thanks to the brilliance of our brain. All of these processes become programmed in our brain, so it can send signals to our body to move in the right way. You don't really have to focus on the way you type on the keyboard and the mechanics of typing – your fingers know what they are doing, so you can concentrate on the work project that you are trying to finish instead. That is what we call – being on autopilot. To be on autopilot means to do things that you usually do on a daily basis, without thinking about them. Hasn't it ever happened to you? You know, to find out about something you have done, but have absolutely no clue when or how. Have you ever wondered why is that? It is because most of the time we do things on autopilot, and doing something automatically means that we don't really pay attention. Did I plug the iron off? Where are my keys? "Sorry, you were saying...?" – do these questions ring a bell? Of course, they do. A study has shown that almost half of the time or nearly 47% of our days to be exact, people's minds wander. That's when your brain turns the autopilot on, so you can safely continue with your task.

Jon Kabat Zinn explains it through the story of me. According to him, people take themselves too seriously, usually because they think that there is someone to take seriously. Then, we create our own stories, or as he says – the story of me. In our stories, we are the main characters and we let 'the supporting roles' in, by interacting with other people. But people forget that it is all a simple construction. There is no me. If we start taking apart each layer like 'am I my name', 'am I my age', 'am I my thoughts', we will see how none of these things make us who we are. According to Zinn, not even our genetic inheritance makes us who we are, since through a different diet and a practice of meditation we can surely express our genes differently. So who am I exactly? When we come to the point of asking ourselves that question, we can then realize the phenomenon called selfing. Selfing is running the narrative of the story of me, and after some time of running our stories in our minds, our brain forms a default mode, and certain regions of our brain become in charge of it. So, when we experience our world through this story mode or default mode, we take information from the outer world, we process it through the filter of how we see things, and then we add our interpretations. Think of it this way. Let's say you are outside and the weather is hot. But you don't see it that way since everything is a part of your story of me. To you, the high temperatures are merely a sign that the summer is coming, which automatically triggers the default mode and you start thinking about the fact that you have to wash all your summer clothes, that you have to buy new sandals, maybe you start thinking about where to go swimming that summer, etc. That is how we run our stories, and the worst part is that we can do this even while driving. That is the autopilot. That is the default mode that our brain switches to. Don't get me wrong, there is nothing wrong with thinking about buying shorts or going on vacation. What is wrong, is the fact that we limit ourselves to only experience the world through the default mode.

So, now you must wonder how will mindfulness help? Mindfulness can light up the other parts of the brain, where there is no story of me. The parts that make us stay conscious and fully present, so we can be aware of every second of our time. Mindfulness will help you switch from auto to manual, so you can be more effective in what you do. Imagine you are cooking dinner and now you are chopping vegetables. If you think about the stressful work thing you have tomorrow, you are more likely to cut your finger, because your brain allowed visual perceptions of the story of me to interfere. On the other hand, if you are mindful about what you are doing and, let's say, focus on the way the red peppers smell when you cut them into strips, you will not only be more effective and enjoy cooking dinner, you will also be less stressed. Doing things mindfully will make you more flexible and ready to respond to the world.

Think it's impossible to achieve such a calm state of mind? Check out the next chapter.

Chapter 4: Cross Your Legs

There are many different types of meditation out there. Spiritual or secular, the bottom line is that each one of them is designed to, among other things, help the practitioner relax and relieve him from stress and anxiety. Some of them require the person to be religious, some types involve repeating a mantra, and there is also a type that only requires from the practitioner to simply be. That type is called mindfulness meditation.

The formal way to become mindful is through the practice of mindfulness meditation. This type of meditation may be derived from the 2,500-year old Buddhist practice, but it is modified, non-spiritual, and based on tons of research. What makes this type of meditation different from the others, is the fact that it doesn't try to enlighten us or makes us different somehow. Through the practice of mindfulness meditation, people can get in touch with the mindfulness inside of them – the awareness that lies within all of us but simply needs to be awakened. Becoming mindful is not learning to think the right way like many may think; becoming mindful simply means becoming aware of your thinking. Only by achieving complete awareness, we can dispute the negativity and move towards a healthier and much happier life. Becoming mindful means being happy.

Preparing For Meditation

Sit down, cross your legs, shut your eyes, breathe in, and wait for the miracle to happen, right? Most of the people who want to become mindful start off the wrong way. You cannot simply force yourself to meditate. You need to give it some time. You need to train your mind to become able to meditate. After all, mindfulness meditation is a practice. And just like any other practice, it requires training. Let's say you want to learn to play tennis. You cannot just buy rackets, a few balls and a pair of tennis shoes and meet a professional player on the court. You need to practice and practice until you actually learn how to play. The same rule applies to playing football, playing the piano, or even making cocktails as a bartender. Every job or sport or technique that you are not familiar with, requires practice. Then, how is meditation any different? If you think that you can simply force your mind to focus, you are so wrong. I don't mean to frighten or discourage you, but only to prepare you for the inevitable.

Meditation is not a performance. It is not something you sit down and get over with. It is a practice that requires a strong will, determination, and patience. Think of it like swimming. Remember when you were little and had all of those floatation devices? No one had jumped into the ocean and simply knew how to swim. We all had to spend some time struggling. Depending on how determined they are, some learn sooner than others. But once you learn, you know it. You may not have been swimming for years, but once you jump into a pool you will know what to do. The same goes with meditation. You may struggle at first, but once you learn how to do it, no one can take that away from you.

So, how to start? Is there a certain pattern that needs to be followed? Like I said, meditation requires practice, and each practice requires preparation. Here is how you can prepare yourself for the practice of mindfulness meditation:

Be Determined. Unless you are really determined to spend some time failing until you actually succeed, don't start meditating. No one was able to achieve a balanced state of mind after the first attempt, and neither will you.

Take a Shower. Many say that enjoying a soothing bath or taking a shower before meditating is extremely helpful. If you think about it, it really makes sense. The fresh and clean feeling that you get after a shower will relax you and may easily get you in the mood for meditating.

Choose Your Location. It doesn't matter if you decide to do it outside or indoors. The point is that your meditating spot is neat, clean and most importantly, a quiet place where you will not be disturbed. It needs to be clean and bright. Your cluttered room is definitely not the place for it. Clean it up, light up a scented candle and make your meditation spot beautiful.

Be Comfortable. Comfort plays a huge part of the process of meditating. You cannot do it if you are cold or sweating. Make sure that you wear comfortable, loose clothes that will not cause discomfort. If it is cold, have a blanket nearby. If it's hot, turn the air-conditioning on, or if you want to meditate outside, try not to do it in the middle of the day.

Make Sure You Will Not Be Distracted. Your iphone and meditation are not well combined. Make sure you will turn your phone off and get rid of other distractions that may interfere with the process of meditating. If you meditate at home, tell your family in advance about your practice, so you will not be bothered.

Imagine. The final outcome that you want to receive by meditating is very important. Use it as an inspiration. Before each practice, spend some time imagining what you will feel like when you finally get to be rewarded with the benefits of mindfulness. The visualizing part is very important, as it will give you strength to overcome the first disappointing attempts.

Learning the Right Posture

The cornerstone of any meditation type really, is the posture that the practitioner takes. Although there are many ways to meditate, and you can do it on your fancy meditation cushion, while sitting on the floor, on the couch, while lying down, or even walking, every one of them requires you to take a certain posture. However, to get to the part where you can meditate while lying on your bed, you first need to master the basic posture. The basic posture is the one you imagine when someone tells you they're meditating. You know, the one when the person is seated with his legs crossed and with his arms on his knees. That is *the lotus posture*. The lotus posture is the best way to start meditating, and that is why experts recommend it to beginners. Here is how you can adjust it the right way:

Sit Down. Experts don't really recommend cushions for beginners since they might distract them at first, so it is better to do it on the floor since it is more productive if you have a flat seat in the beginning.

Adjust the Right Foot. Take your right foot and place it on your left thigh. Try to do it as close to the hip as you can. Keep your left ankle straight.

Adjust the Left Foot. Take your left foot and place it on your right thigh. Try to do it as close to the hip as you can. Keep your right ankle straight.

If this is too much for you and you don't feel very comfortable with the real lotus posture, you can always just cross your legs the way you usually do. Many people meditate that way.

Straighten the Spine. Don't hunch down. Your spine must be straight, but not too much, as you don't want to be stiff.

Relax the Shoulders. Strengthening the spine doesn't mean that you should have tensed shoulders. Make sure they rest comfortably.

Drop the Chin. Just like your shoulders, your head must be also comfortable throughout the whole practice. Drop the chin a little bit, but don't overdo it.

Placing Your Hands. First, extend your arms over your thighs. Then, place your hands just above your knees. This is the perfect place for them as you don't want to be loose or stiff. Your palms should be facing upward.

Close Your Eyes. Yes, some people meditate with loosened eyelids, but if you are just starting out, it is best to keep your eyes closed.

Step-By-Step Practice

Practicing to become mindful the formal way, through the act of meditation, isn't as intimidating as it may seem to you at this point. Struggling to achieve a balance, becoming aware, and getting rid of the distracting thoughts is normal. The most important thing is to remember to lose your judging attitude. After all, that is what being mindful is all about, right?

Take your time with this practice and don't rush. Go through the steps, slowly, one by one, until you learn them by heart. You may fail at first, but what you will get at the end, now that is something worth trying for.

Step 1: Settle

A very important part of practicing mindfulness meditation is to take a few moments to settle before you actually start. This is especially important if you had a busy day or you feel strange about meditating. First of all, get comfortable. Roll your head or do whatever does the trick for you, and whatever helps you to knock down the tension. Sit for a moment and try to detach yourself from the flood of thoughts. To do so, try to 'slide' through your thoughts. You know, the same way you slide your photos on your iPhone. Move from one thought to another, until you feel the pressure lessening. When you feel them dancing around your head, it is time to begin.

Step 2: Take a Deep Breath

Breathing is a very important component of the formal practice of mindfulness, which means that you should really make sure to do it the right way. Try to put your sole attention to it. Take a deep breath by saying 'inhale' in your mind. Pay attention to the air that enters your mouth, how it travels through your throat and fills your lungs. Hold it there for a second. Slowly, say 'exhale' in your mind and let the air out. By taking deep breaths you can relax not only your mind but your body, as well.

There is a way of practicing mindfulness that is called 'breathing meditation'. The practitioner puts his focus on the deep breaths throughout the entire practice. He tries not to get caught up in his thoughts by forcing himself to be aware of the breathing. You can try this too, but if you are just starting out, I highly suggest you go through all of the steps, first.

Step 3: Scan Your Body

The body scan technique is also a type of mindfulness meditation that can be practiced on its own. It also starts with settling and taking a couple of deep breaths as a way to relax the mind and put yourself in a mood for meditating. The breathing part here isn't there as a tool where you put the attention, but simply a way to lessen the tension before you start meditating.

By scanning your body, you will establish body awareness that will train your mind how to keep the focus on a single thing for as long as you feel like it. Through this practice, you will also learn how to easily shift the attention from one thing to another.

To start, divide your body into small parts: arms, legs, head, etc. Take the time to really feel each part separately. How do they feel? What is their connection with one another? Now, take each part and divide it into even smaller parts. For instance, take the arm and divide it into hand, forearm, elbow, etc. Try to feel these parts as well. Think about their function. Now, divide them into even smaller parts if you can. Like, for example, take the hand and divide it into fingers, knuckles, etc. Think about each of these parts separately. You can do this either with your entire body or with a single part. The point is to shift your attention, while disputing the distracting thoughts.

Step 4: Turn On Your Senses

Your senses should play a pretty important role while practicing mindfulness meditation. They are the thing that allows you to become mindful really, so, you should also try to be mindful of them, as well. What do I mean by that? During mindfulness meditation, it is not enough to simply note that you have the senses and be aware of their function. You should become mindful about each of them, at that given moment. Let's start with what you can hear. Place your focus on the sounds, even if there aren't any. If you are in your room and you can't hear anything, focus on the silence. If you meditate outdoors, focus on the chirping of the birds, the chattering, the distant traffic sounds, etc. Now, focus on what you can smell. Perhaps you have a scented candle in your room. Or, if you are outside, focus on the smell of the grass, maybe there are flowers, or maybe an appealing smell from someone's kitchen is spreading through the air. Do this with each of your senses, separately.

Step 5: Spend Some Time with Your Thoughts

It is in our human nature to think. Don't think that meditating can help you stop that from happening, because that is simply impossible. What you can achieve through the practice of mindfulness meditation, though, is to train your mind to choose between those thoughts, and to get rid of the ones that may cause you stress or may bring your mood down. But, in order to do so, you need to spend some time with your thoughts, first.

Closely observe your thoughts, just remember not to get into details. First, you need to just acknowledge the existence of your thoughts. Simply imagine them circling around your head. You can see them all, but you don't engage.

After observing them, you get a clear picture which ones of your thoughts have a negative impact on you and which ones cheer you up. Naturally, we want to get rid of the negativity. Before you do that, however, you need to realize that you are not your thoughts, and you have the power to let some of them go. So, do it. Try to put your focus solely on the positive ones, to train your mind to learn how to release the negativity.

Step 6: Without Judging

Remember, mindfulness is a nonjudgmental practice. Just like you shouldn't judge the things you hear, see, and experience, you also shouldn't judge yourself. This may be a tough one, especially in the beginning, but try not to be too harsh on yourself. Sooner or later, your mind will wander off. It is normal, and trust me when I tell you this, it has happened even to the meditation gurus, so don't judge yourself for not being able to be in control all the time.

Step 7: Return

When you get distracted by a stream of thoughts, simply go back to the beginning. Remember Super Mario? You make a mistake, you lose a life, you start over. Think of this practice that way. Each time you make a mistake and get tangled up in some of your thoughts, simply tell yourself that is okay, and go back to step number 1.

Step 8: End It

No one will recommend you to simply open your eyes and stand up after a meditation. After being in such calm state of mind, it is important to slowly open your eyes and return to your surroundings. Stretch your legs, wiggle your toes, roll your head and shoulders, and stand up.

This step-by-step formal practice of mindfulness will help you become in control of your thoughts and feelings. It will strengthen your focus and make you able to concentrate even on the tiniest details, so you can become able to see what you couldn't before.

Chapter 5: Squeezing Mindfulness In

This modern world we live in forces us to move at such a fast pace which allows our lives to basically pass us by. Like we are brought to this world and put on a fast track; we move so fast that we are unable to see what's going on around us clearly. Think about it for a second. Your days are filled with busy schedules and activities that you can barely squeeze some time in, to have a proper lunch. Not to mention the health problems that we support by leading this overloaded, in-the-fast-lane, busy lifestyle. But how do we slow the pace? Is it even possible not to speed in this crazy world? Although it may seem to you that your world will fall apart if you just take a break, it really won't. No, I am not talking about telling your boss you've decided to take a break from work and lose your job, but to take a break from your cluttered mind. Wouldn't it be great if you could just enjoy the beauty of the small things in life, without being constantly interrupted by some flow of thoughts?

As you've all learned by now, the practice of mindfulness can indeed help you achieve that. But how do you find the time for this practice? How to become mindful if you live a super busy life? When can you find the time for meditating? In spite of the business in our lives, a person that truly wants to live in equilibrium, can surely find a way to get rid of these excuses and make some room for practicing mindfulness meditation:

First thing in the morning. Setting the alarm 10 minutes earlier will definitely not affect the quality of your sleep, but 10-minute morning meditations can definitely improve the quality of your life. At first, it may seem like a struggle to try to focus first thing in the morning, but give it a time. After some time, these morning meditations will become a routine, just like washing your face or brushing the teeth.

While walking. Even though it is true that walking meditation is a bit more challenging than meditating in the lotus posture, as it requires an increased amount of patience, it is also true that if you practice it, you can master it. Don't waste your time stressing over things or replaying scenarios in your mind while walking, use that time to practice mindfulness instead. It doesn't matter if you are walking to work or going grocery shopping. Slow down the pace and be in the moment. Feel your muscles stretch, focus on the way your feet touch the ground, try to feel the sensations, and simply be.

Small, but frequent. There is no doubt that 20 minutes of meditating are ideal, but the truth is, you cannot always spare that much time for this practice. This is the main excuse why people avoid meditating, but what they don't know, is that breaking the meditation practice into small fragments, can be just as beneficial as meditating straight for a half an hour is. Let's take the time you spend working, as an example. There is no time for mindfulness meditation from 9 to 5, right? Well, wrong. You can spare 5 minutes of your lunch break for meditating, you can do it for a minute or two on your bathroom breaks, you can take a few moments to breathe while you are alone in the office, etc. Meditating a couple of times while at work, even if it is only for a minute or two, can have a huge impact on your progress.

Schedule it. Meditation should be just as important, as any other task in your life, so make sure not to skip it. Set a reminder for your mindfulness practice and make it non-negotiable. You cannot choose to have a coffee with your friend instead. It is also suggested that you choose a time and stick with it. This will make things a lot easier.

Attach it. Many people will agree that finding an *anchor* for the practice, can help you become mindful. Attaching the mindfulness practice to something will help you form a meditating routine. I suggest you to do it each time you finish something. For instance, after you shop for groceries, sit in your car, and take a minute or two to meditate. After your work day is over, do the same. Try it after you finish cooking, after you clean your house, etc. Taking a few moments to clear your mind after each completed task can be quite beneficial.

Informally

The most amazing thing about becoming mindful is that you don't have to be always meditating in order to practice. Remember how I said that mindfulness meditation is the formal way of practicing? That means that you can also practice mindfulness informally. The informal practice of mindfulness is actually everything we do on a daily basis. Although meditation can surely help you in bringing balance to your mind, it will not be as successful if you choose to pollute your brain when you are not lotus-seated.

Mindfulness is not only a state of mind, but it is also a way of life. To live mindfully means to be mindful throughout the whole day. The informal practice of mindfulness helps you achieve just that. Doing things with awareness and without judging, you can truly get to enjoy each moment, without losing a second of your day.

When you wake up, try not to rush into the toilet, or think about how much you would want to go back to sleep. Instead, try to find beauty in the morning. Focus on the chirping of the birds or the weather. Open the window and try to feel the warmth or the breeze on your skin.

Eat mindfully. While eating, try not to read the news, watch TV, or text. Instead, try to savor every bite. Focus on the way your body responds, your desire to eat. Focus on the tempting smell of the food and its delightful taste.

When traveling to work, try to be mindful of what is going on around you. Don't get caught up in your thoughts – be present instead.

Try to do everything mindfully. Each task can be performed mindfully. Brushing teeth, cooking, cleaning, reading, etc. Try to be fully aware of everything you do.

Chapter 6: Overcoming the Obstacles

The reason why I chose to write this chapter is because I am really frustrated with how other authors, and media in general, present the practice of mindfulness. I mainly blame them for the fact that there are so many people who quit meditating. It's not their fault, they are told what to do in order to receive the benefits of mindfulness, but after a couple of attempts, when they see that nothing is really happening, understandably, they quit. There are tons of books about mindfulness meditation that will try to convince you why meditating is good for you. They will try to teach you the oh-so-simple technique and think you are provided with what you need to embark this stress-relieving journey. But, to find a book that will tell you that practicing mindfulness isn't a walk in the park, now that is rare.

So, I've decided to include this chapter, not because I want you to feel intimidated by this practice, but simply to warn you not to start your path to becoming mindful, until you are truly ready. Mindfulness can be a tricky habit to establish, and along the way, there will be obstacles to overcome.

You will be irritated. The inevitable part of beginning to meditate is, of course, irritation. Anything from distracting smell, a loud noise coming from the neighbor's house, or wearing uncomfortable clothes can make you feel irritated and interrupt the practice of mindfulness. The best way to ensure that the irritation will not be a part of your practice is by preparing yourself well. Now, you will probably need to spend a couple of times meditating irritated to find the perfect way to do it, but don't give up.

You will feel restless. Since you are probably not used to sitting in a lotus position, chances are, it will bother you. The idea of sitting still is usually quite a challenge, so people try too hard to do it the right way. Using too much effort to sit relaxed is rather contradictory. My advice here is – don't try. If you have to scratch your leg, go ahead. The whole point is to sit relaxed, not to be tensed. Try to have that in mind, and try to do it, not the way this guidebook says, but the way that suits you the most. After all, we're all different.

You will have doubts. Thinking 'this doesn't work for me' is quite destructive. Reading all those stories where people achieved serenity and equilibrium through meditation should only inspire you. They shouldn't be used as a comparison to the way you practice mindfulness. Believing that you will never get to taste these benefits because you don't have what it takes, is really the worst possible way to start this practice. Instead, think 'why not?'. Why shouldn't you become mindful? What makes you so different than the others? Try to have a more positive approach to mindfulness and remember to give it some time. It can take a while.

You will be bored. Chances are, sooner or later (before you master it, of course) you will find the practice of mindfulness, to be boring. Trying to avoid the distracting thoughts through the formal practice may seem like an extremely uninteresting thing to do at first. To make sure that this will not be a problem, each time before you start mindfulness meditation, remind yourself of what you want to achieve in the end. What is your desired outcome? Why did you start practicing mindfulness in the first place? Telling yourself why you are doing it, will give you strength to endure that initial phase of becoming mindful.

You will be impatient. People usually start this practice and wait for the 'miracle' to happen. Being impatient to become mindful will only do the opposite. Instead of tapping your fingers, why not prepare yourself? Only by truly knowing that it will take some time and patience, you can start receiving the rewards that mindfulness offer. Don't start this practice, unless you are absolutely sure that this will not be a problem for you.

Chapter 7: Staying Behind the Wheel

'How to know if I am doing it right?' is something that new practitioners ask themselves. How to know if you are behind the wheel and have already gained control over your thoughts and emotions? How to know if you are not? If you ask a meditation guru if there is something that you can do in order to see if you have become mindful or not, you will most likely get the same answer – to simply be, and that when you start getting the benefits that mindfulness has to offer, you will surely know it. Although it is truth that getting wrapped up in the concept will give you only more to think about, I cannot say that I agree with that completely. If you ask me, I believe that there is a way for you to know if the hours of practicing have started to pay out.

As a beginner, it can be confusing to determine if you are really being mindful or if you are simply aware. Sure, there isn't a magical device that will show your progress, but that doesn't mean that there isn't a way for you to see if you are making any. Here are some tips that you can try, to see if you hold the wheel:

Write your feelings down. Keep an emotional diary to see if the practice of mindfulness has made you feel better. Review it after 7 days and see if there is a progress. If there is, don't toss that notebook away, but continue tracking it. You will most likely see how each week your mood will only rise. I suggest using the scale of 1-10 for this.

Download an app. It may sound silly, but today there are tons of insanely helpful apps. There are even those that can track your mindfulness.

Watch how you perform the tasks you usually hate. If you see that they don't bother you as much as they did before, then, that is a clear indicator that you are on the right path.

In case you still can't tell whether your mindfulness is working even after implementing the previous tricks, then I suggest you make a pause. Stop with your mindfulness for 2 days and go back to the old you. Watch your behavior closely. If you are in a low mood and stressed, then you know the answer to your question.

Once you get the answer to your question and are sure that you have become mindful, the last tip I wanna give you is to stay behind the wheel and control your emotions and thoughts.

Conclusion

Before you go, I just wanted to say thank you for purchasing my book.

You could have picked from dozens of other books on the same topic but you took a chance and chose this one.

So, a HUGE thanks to you for getting this book and for reading all the way to the end.

Now I wanted to ask you for a small favor. **Could you please take just a few minutes to leave a review for this book on Amazon?**

This feedback will help me continue to write the type of books that will help you get the results you want. So if you enjoyed it, please let me know! (-:

Made in the USA
Middletown, DE
07 February 2019